圣贤的礼物

[美]欧·亨利 著
陈月红 黎智林 副主编
朱振武 主编

欧·亨利短篇小说精选

名家导读有声版

英汉对照·插图版

華東理工大學出版社
EAST CHINA UNIVERSITY OF SCIENCE AND TECHNOLOGY PRESS

图书在版编目(CIP)数据

圣贤的礼物：欧·亨利短篇小说精选：英汉对照·名家导读有声版 / 朱振武主编. —上海：华东理工大学出版社, 2019.2
(经典短篇双语阅读)
ISBN 978-7-5628-5467-8

Ⅰ.①圣… Ⅱ.①朱… Ⅲ.①英语－汉语－对照读物②短篇小说－小说集－美国－近代 Ⅳ.①H319.4：I

中国版本图书馆CIP数据核字(2018)第093321号

策划编辑 / 信 艳
责任编辑 / 信 艳
装帧设计 / 风信子
插　　画 / 李 丹
出版发行 / 华东理工大学出版社有限公司
地址：上海市梅陇路130号，200237
电话：021-64250306
网址：www.ecustpress.cn
邮箱：zongbianban@ecustpress.cn
印　　刷 / 上海盛通时代印刷有限公司
开　　本 / 890mm × 1240mm 1/32
印　　张 / 8.125
字　　数 / 225千字
版　　次 / 2019年2月第1版
印　　次 / 2019年2月第1次
定　　价 / 39.80元

扫一扫，听有声导读

走进上海师范大学

博士生导师朱振武教授的

文学课堂

聆听该音频，你可以获知：

1. 欧·亨利的传奇人生及其写作风格。
2. 《廿载之后》精彩导读。
3. 阅读经典的当下意义。

经典阅读的当下意义

朱振武

有个学生要考我的研究生，我回信给她说，考我的研究生，要能够静下心来读书，不枉过三年，不要只顾蝇头微利，不要陷入琐碎，不要流于肤浅，立足在眼前，但立志要高远，至少要做一个文化人，而不是个只顾眼前利益的小市民，渐次达到人生较高的境界。这个学生很坚决，她回信说，读研的目的不仅是学习更多的知识，更重要的是充实人生，完善人格，提高自己的精神境界。回答得很好，正是我要的答案，后来她得偿所愿，心无旁骛地读起书来，再后来表现出很强的后劲。

要否读书，读书重要与否，重要到什么程度，这些在不久前被看作是只有白痴才会问的问题在当下还真成了问题。我们的孔老夫子曾说，不读诗，无以言。十七世纪英国哲人弗朗西斯·培根说的好，读书使人充实，不常读书者须欺世有术，始能无知而显有知。人之才智但有滞碍，无不可读适当之书使之顺畅。读书，首要的是读什么书呢？当然是读经典著作。什么是经典？常念为经，常数为典，是为经典。经典就是经得起反复重复的文本，其之所以得以如此就在于其丰厚的文化蕴含，就在于我们每次对之重温都能从中开掘出熏染和涤荡我们灵魂的东西。

同样一篇文章或一个理论，能经得起人反复咀嚼。经典还具有不可超越性，更不是我们眼前这些急功近利的东西所能替代的。著名电视导演张纪中说："经典是不能超越的。你可以在他旁边再垒一座山，却无法超越这座山。"经典就是这样的一些作品，常读常新，且不会过时或落伍。历史文化学者易中天说得好，经典就是最有价值、最有意义的著作。他还引用中国那句老话教育大家，"取法其上，得乎其中。取法其中，得乎其下。""取法其上"，对于我们读书人来说，当然就是阅读经典。

有个读者在网上留帖子说，没有读意大利的伊塔洛·卡尔维诺的《为什么读经典》，那是旷世奇憾。旷世不旷世不敢说，遗憾是肯定有的。卡尔维诺对经典的阐发却是深刻，他认为，经典作品是一些产生某种特殊影响的书，他们要么本身以难忘的方式给我们的想象力打下印记，要么乔装成个人或集体的无意识隐藏在深层记忆中，经典作品是一本不会耗尽它要向你说的一切东西的书。他还认为，经典作品是这样的一些书，它们带着先前解释的气息走向我们，背后拖着它们经过文化或多种文化（或只是多种语言和风俗）时留下的足迹。这些话说得真是深刻，我曾经在一次关于经典阅读的讲座上稍事夸张地说：经典文学是这样的书：

它是使没有头脑的人变得有头脑，没有文化的人变得有文化的书，是使肤浅之徒变得稳重、呆板之人变得诙谐、迟滞之人变得睿智、短视之人变得远见、丑陋之人变得俊拔、狭隘之人变得宽容、妒忌变得羡慕、贪婪变得节制、吝啬变得慷慨、苛刻变得宽容、卑微变得高贵、猥琐变得雍容、空虚变得充实、奢靡变得简朴、情调低俗变得品位高雅、百无聊赖变得丰富多彩的书，是那些让你得到调整、使你得到憩息、能够与你沟通、可以帮你排遣郁闷的书，是能够为你提供生活坐标的书，是可以让你放松身心、宣泄激愤的书，是使你保持坦荡荡免于常戚戚的书，是使你高出只掌握某种一般技能的人的书，是使你摆脱生存尴尬、尽享人生乐趣的书，是使你懂得一个人为什么要活着的书，是使高级动物有别于其他动物的书。

有个听众问我什么时候读经典，我戏谑地回答说："当你神情抑郁、兴趣寡淡的时候，当你情场失意、官场失落的时候，当你挫败连连、股市大跌的时候，当你参透人生、看破红尘的时候，当你失业下岗的时候，当你屡试不中的时候，当你穷得只剩下钱的时候，当你辗转反侧、夜不成寐、茶饭无思、百无聊赖的时候，当你不知道人为什么而活着的时候，当你不知道你到底有什么用处的时候，当你在充满喧哗与骚动的都市里无处逃逸的时候，不要想入非非，不要萌生他想，尽情享受经典阅读带给你的乐趣吧！"

为什么要读经典？易中天说得好，就是因为能从经典中读人生，读智慧，读社会。我颇以为然，所以，每天没有不看书的时候，没有不接触经典的时候，否则就觉得怅然若失，缺少了根基，没了底气，丢了自信。

这套四卷本的"美国名家短篇小说精选"所收作家作品就是前面所说的那样的经典之作，很具代表性，基本上让我们看到了美国短篇小说的整体面貌，而且这些作品仍与当下有着很强的意义关联，因此，其读者群也比较宽广。画龙点睛般的导读、简练严谨的注释和紧扣源语的译文为读者体会作品主旨意蕴、创作技巧和学习、欣赏原文文本提供了很大便利。

这套书的撰译者都是在高校里专门从事英美文学教学和研究的人员，主编是上海师范大学的朱振武，副主编是上海师范大学的冯德河、蓝云春，山东大学的高静，三峡大学的陈月红、杨鸿雁、黎智林、任慧芝，以及上海大学外国语学院的张惠英。大家在多年的教研实践中达成一个共识：一个不读经典作品的人是不完整的人，没有一定的英美文学经典作品的阅读量，一个人的英语水平是不可能达到较高层次的，他在这个方面的整体文化素养肯定是有缺陷的。因此，我们向各位读者奉上这套“美国名家短篇小说精选”。

欧·亨利其人

冯德河

如果您在浩若烟海的书籍中挑中了此书，相信您对欧·亨利（O·Henry, 1862—1910）之名一定不感到陌生。《财神与爱神》《圣贤的礼物》《警察与赞美诗》《最后一片常春藤叶》《带家具的出租屋》……总有个故事曾扰动您的心弦：或让您垂泪，或让您苦笑，或让您唏嘘，或让您捧腹。这或许会让您坐下来，静静地捧一盏香茗，伴您重温那曾经的感动。

如果您恰是初读此书，劝您不要马上离开，因为不经意间您或许就与这位世界短篇小说之王擦肩而过了。《绿房门》《廿载之后》《命运之路》《红毛酋长的赎金》《感恩节的两位先生》……终有个故事能让您体味到一种别样的人生。或立或卧、或行或停，在骚动与喧哗的生活中，您需要一次心灵的涤净。

威廉·西德尼·波特（William Sidney Porter，1898 年改名为 William Sydney Poter），1862 年出生于美国北卡罗来纳州，欧·亨利是他的笔名。

像许多伟大作家一样，欧·亨利的一生也是命运多舛。三岁之时，父母辞世，由祖母和姑妈抚养长大；束发之年，因家庭贫困被迫中学辍学；之后，他唱过歌、演过戏、当过记者、干过出纳、做过药剂师，也做过绘图员。丰富的职业经历使其对美国市井平民的生活十分谙熟。二十五岁时，他不顾女友父母反对，毅然与阿索尔·埃斯蒂斯私奔并结婚，但十年后结发之妻不幸罹病去世，他也染上了酗酒的恶习。后来他与莎拉·林德赛·科尔曼结婚，因酗酒赌博、挥霍无度而致债台高筑，两年后离婚。坎坷的婚姻经历使他对家庭与爱情多了番与众不同的体会。

1896年，他被控盗用公款，为避牢狱之灾他逃往洪都拉斯。逃亡期间，因妻子病危不得不返回美国，旋即被捕入狱五年。服刑期间，他开始认真地进行小说创作，并以欧·亨利为笔名发表。三年后，因表现良好他提前获释。谁曾想，锒铛入狱三载，一旦脱身囹圄，寂寂无名的罪犯威廉·西德尼·波特很快就成了享誉全美的小说家欧·亨利，他的成名宛如他的小说结局，出人意表！

此后，欧·亨利的创作一发不可收拾，佳作频出，名利双收。出狱后第二年，他移居纽约走上职业作家之路。他一生创作了数百篇脍炙人口的短篇小说，被誉为美国短篇小说之父，与法国的莫泊桑、俄国的契诃夫并称世界三大短篇小说之王。但是，由于长期的艰苦创作，加之酗酒无度、生活不节制，他的健康受到了严重损害。1910年6月，他在创作最后一篇短篇小说《梦》时病倒，随后溘然仙逝，留下了大量债务。其命运之曲折令人扼腕，其创作之丰硕令人景仰，其艺术之瑰丽令人陶醉。

欧·亨利小说题材广泛，既有对美国西部生活的书写，也有对拉美异域风情的描绘，当然最重要的还是对美国都市市井小人物的命运观照。小说中权贵的利欲熏心与尔虞我诈、寒门的穷途落魄与悲欢离合，无不揭露了当时美国社会的人情冷暖与世态炎凉，但在贫富冲突、美丑对照、善恶交锋中，欧·亨利让读者看到他对单纯人性的追求、对真诚爱情的颂扬。欧·亨利小说艺术也别具一格。且不论他耳熟能详的"欧·亨利式结局"，也不说他诙谐幽默的语言、针针见血的讽刺，单就其对语言节奏、韵律的把控，宛若行云流水，就值得静下心来仔细品味。

欧·亨利坎坷不平的一生和他异彩纷呈的作品互为参照，从其作品中您可领略他传奇般的人生经历，从其命运中您可更深刻地品味其作品的人生蕴涵，所以，无论您是重温还是初读，无论您是为英语学习还是为娱乐消遣，我们相信它都不会让您失望。当然，其中鱼鲁豕亥之处，亦请不吝斤斧！

目 录

O Henry

1862 – 1910

O Henry, original name william Sydndy Porter,

was an American short story writer.

His stories are known for

their surprise endings.

After Twenty Years
廿载之后

在西部打拼发迹的鲍勃，千辛万苦，千里迢迢，冒着被捕的危险，赶赴二十年前与老友的约会，没想到却被逮了个正着，锒铛入狱，而把他投入监狱的正是他二十年来念兹在兹的发小吉米。

欧·亨利的小说一向以出人意表的结尾著称，但这篇故事的结尾还是让人唏嘘半晌。身为警察的吉米，当看出赶来赴约的老友就是警方通缉的罪犯时，抓与不抓就成了问题。我们可能会觉得吉米忒无情，觉得他完全可以佯装不知，放老友一马。但转念一想，我们就会发现，这涉及做人和做事的一个底线问题。人当然要重然诺，讲信用。一诺千金，一言九鼎，在诚信面前，金钱如粪土，诚信之于人的重要性毋庸置疑。“三杯吐然诺，五岳倒为轻”，气壮山河，气冲牛斗，这等守诺是何等气概！“长存抱柱信，岂上望夫台！”这是何等坚贞，令那些见异思迁、朝秦暮楚、朝三暮四、唯利是图的宵小之辈相形见绌，无所遁形。然而，诚信与守诺，并不是没有原则甚或没有条件的一味愚忠。在然诺与道义之间，我们肯定应该选择道义。在守诚与守法之间，我们肯定选择守法。不论做什么事，守住做人的底线，不触犯法律的红线，这才是真正的人性和理性。情，不能大于法；义，不能高于法；忠，也不能强于法；任何事情都不能凌驾于法律之上。而作为警察的吉米，如果玩忽职守，放走罪犯，他就既没有守住做人的底线，又触犯了法律的底线，他就既不是合格的人，也不是合格的公民，更不是合格的警察。欧·亨利被称作“美国的莫泊桑”，他的短篇小说之所以受到世界各国读者的喜欢，其艺术成就是一方面，其多维的思想蕴含和丰富的启示意义也是一个重要方面。

The policeman on the beat moved up the avenue impressively. The impressiveness was habitual and not for show, for spectators were few. The time was barely 10 o'clock at night, but chilly gusts of wind with a taste of rain in them had well-nigh depeopled the streets.

Trying doors as he went, twirling his club ① with many intricate and artful movements, turning now and then to cast his watchful eye adown the pacific thoroughfare, the officer, with his stalwart form and slight swagger, made a fine picture of a guardian of the peace. The vicinity ② was one that kept early hours. Now and then you might see the lights of a cigar store or of an all-night lunch counter; but the majority of the doors belonged to business places that had long since been closed.

When about midway of a certain block the policeman suddenly slowed his walk. In the doorway of a darkened hardware store a man leaned, with an unlighted cigar in his mouth. As the policeman walked up to him the man spoke up quickly.

"It's all right, officer," he said, reassuringly. "I'm just waiting for a friend. It's an appointment made twenty years ago. Sounds a little funny to you, doesn't it? Well, I'll explain if you'd like to make certain it's all straight. About that long ago there used to be a restaurant where this store stands—'Big Joe' Brady's restaurant."

"Until five years ago," said the policeman. "It was torn down then."

The man in the doorway struck a match and lit his cigar.

---

① club *n.* 警棍 ② vicinity *n.* 附近，邻近地区

警察正一本正经地沿街巡逻。这种一本正经乃习惯使然，并非作秀，因为观者寥寥。时间还不到夜里十点，但冷风阵阵，雨意渐浓，街上已没什么行人了。

警察体格壮伟，阔步昂首，一边走一边不停地推试检查着两边的店门，手里的警棍转得眼花缭乱，双目还不时地扫视着宁静的大街，形成了一幅绝妙的平安卫士图。这里的店关门都早，偶尔能瞥见雪茄店或通宵便利店的几盏灯光，但大部分店面都是早早就关门打烊的。

走到一个街区的一半，警察突然放慢了脚步。黑暗的五金店门口，一个男子斜靠着，嘴里叼着一根还未点燃的雪茄。见警察向他走来，他赶忙开口。

“这里没啥事，警官。”那人让人放心地说道。“我就是等个朋友，是二十年前的一个约定。听着有点不可思议，对不？噢，你要是想弄清这的确没啥事，那我解释一下。大约那么久之前，就在这家五金店现在的位置，原来是个饭店——‘大乔布雷迪’餐馆。”

“直到五年前。”警察说。“那时才推倒的。”

门口那人划了根火柴，点燃了嘴里的雪茄。火光映衬出的是一

The light showed a pale, square-jawed face with keen eyes, and a little white scar near his right eyebrow. His scarfpin was a large diamond, oddly set.

"Twenty years ago to-night," said the man, "I dined here at 'Big Joe' Brady's with Jimmy Wells, my best chum[①], and the finest chap in the world. He and I were raised here in New York, just like two brothers, together. I was eighteen and Jimmy was twenty. The next morning I was to start for the West to make my fortune. You couldn't have dragged Jimmy out of New York; he thought it was the only place on earth. Well, we agreed that night that we would meet here again exactly twenty years from that date and time, no matter what our conditions might be or from what distance we might have to come. We figured that in twenty years each of us ought to have our destiny worked out and our fortunes made, whatever they were going to be."

"It sounds pretty interesting," said the policeman. "Rather a long time between meets, though, it seems to me. Haven't you heard from your friend since you left?"

"Well, yes, for a time we corresponded," said the other. "But after a year or two we lost track of each other. You see, the West is a pretty big proposition, and I kept hustling around over it pretty lively. But I know Jimmy will meet me here if he's alive[②],

① my best chum，我最要好的朋友。下文中的 the finest chap（最优秀的老兄）、stanchest old chap（最可靠的老兄），old chap（老兄），old partner（老伙计），good fellow（不错的家伙），old man（老哥们），都是对老友比较亲切又随意的称呼，这些词根据上下文都做了不同的翻译，其实他们在文本中的意思大体是相同的。英文中经常用不同的词来指代人或事，是一种修辞手法。

② if he's alive，如果他活着。下文中的 alive on earth（活在世上）和 still in existence（还健在），其实都是表达"活着"的意思，但上下文中力避单一重复，从而增强了文本的力度和文采。注意此处对这三个表达法的翻译。

张苍白的方形脸膛，双眼敏锐，右眉角上还有块小白疤。他的领带别针上是一颗硕大的钻石，镶嵌得怪怪的。

“二十年前的今晚，”那人说道。“我和我最要好的朋友，世上最优秀的家伙吉米·威尔斯，在这家‘大乔布雷迪’餐馆共进晚餐。我俩都在纽约长大，就像亲哥俩。我十八，吉米二十。我第二天早晨就要动身到西部去圆我的发财梦。你是没法把吉米从纽约拽出来的，他只知道世上有纽约。就这样，那天晚上我俩说定，就在二十年后的此日此时，我们再次相聚于此，无论情况如何，不管路途多远。我们猜想，二十年后，不管具体情况怎样，我们俩总该混出个样了，总该发点财了。”

“听起来确实挺有意思。”警察说。“这中间隔的真是够长的，我看也是！你走后就没有你朋友的音信吗？”

“哦，是啊！我们一度保持着联系。”那人说。“但一两年后，我们彼此就失去了音信。你知道，西部是个大生意场，我整天跑来跑去的，忙乱不堪。但我知道，吉米活着的话定会来这儿见我，因为他一向是最真诚、最可靠的家伙。他绝不会忘记。我今夜千里迢迢赶来，站在这门口等候，只要我的老伙计能来，这一切就都值得。”

for he always was the truest, stanchest old chap in the world. He'll never forget. I came a thousand miles to stand in this door to-night, and it's worth it if my old partner turns up."

The waiting man pulled out a handsome watch, the lids of it set with small diamonds.

"Three minutes to ten," he announced. "It was exactly ten o'clock when we parted here at the restaurant door."

"Did pretty well out West, didn't you?" asked the policeman.

"You bet! I hope Jimmy has done half as well. He was a kind of plodder①, though, good fellow as he was. I've had to compete with some of the sharpest wits going to get my pile. A man gets in a groove in New York. It takes the West to put a razor-edge on him."

The policeman twirled his club and took a step or two.

"I'll be on my way. Hope your friend comes around all right. Going to call time on him sharp?"

"I should say not!" said the other. "I'll give him half an hour at least. If Jimmy is alive on earth he'll be here by that time. So long, officer."

"Good-night, sir," said the policeman, passing on along his beat, trying doors as he went.

There was now a fine, cold drizzle② falling, and the wind had risen from its uncertain puffs into a steady blow. The few foot passengers astir③ in that quarter hurried dismally and silently along with coat collars turned high and pocketed hands. And in

① plodder *n.* 动作慢且不太聪明的人；慢性子的人

② drizzle *n.* 毛毛雨 ③ astir *adj.* 活动的

那人掏出一块漂亮的手表，表盖上镶嵌的小钻石闪闪发光。

“还有三分钟十点。”那人说道。“我们从这家餐馆门口分手时刚好十点。”

“在西部那边混得很不错吧？”警察问。

“你说对了！吉米干得有我一半好就行了。当然，他也很勤奋，是个不错的家伙。有些人聪明绝顶，他们要算计我的钱袋子，我就得和他们斗智斗勇。人在纽约容易墨守成规，他们真应该到西部去历练历练。”

警察转动着警棍，来回踱了几步。

“我得巡逻去了。但愿你那朋友如期赴约。就等到十点吗？”

“那不会。”那人说。“我至少要给他半个钟头。只要还活在世上，吉米那时会来的。再见，警官。”

“再见，先生。”警察说，接着往前巡视去了，一边推试检查着店门。

天下起了毛毛细雨，令人惬意，但寒意渐浓，刚刚的习习微风，现在已很强劲。附近活动的三两行人都衣领高翻，双手插袋，行色匆匆，闷声不语。五金店门口，千里迢迢赶来赴发小之约的男子抽着雪茄，还在等着，他心里实在没底。

the door of the hardware store the man who had come a thousand miles to fill an appointment, uncertain almost to absurdity, with the friend of his youth, smoked his cigar and waited.

About twenty minutes he waited, and then a tall man in a long overcoat, with collar turned up to his ears, hurried across from the opposite side of the street. He went directly to the waiting man.

"Is that you, Bob?" he asked, doubtfully.

"Is that you, Jimmy Wells?" cried the man in the door.

"Bless my heart!" exclaimed the new arrival, grasping both the other's hands with his own. "It's Bob, sure as fate. I was certain I'd find you here if you were still in existence. Well, well, well!—twenty years is a long time. The old restaurant's gone, Bob; I wish it had lasted, so we could have had another dinner there. How has the West treated you, old man?"

"Bully; it has given me everything I asked it for. You've changed lots, Jimmy. I never thought you were so tall by two or three inches."

"Oh, I grew a bit after I was twenty."

"Doing well in New York, Jimmy?"

"Moderately. I have a position in one of the city departments. Come on, Bob; we'll go around to a place I know of, and have a good long talk about old times."

The two men started up the street, arm in arm. The man from the West, his egotism[①] enlarged by success, was beginning to outline the history of his career. The other, submerged in his

① egotism *n.* 自负

那人等了二十多分钟，这时，一个高个头男子从街道对面匆匆赶了过来，他穿着长长的大衣，领子高翻到耳际。他径直走向了那人。

“鲍勃，是你吗？”那人疑惑地问道。

“吉米·威尔斯？是你吗？”站在门口的男子大声喊道。

“谢天谢地！”来人喊道，紧紧地抓住这人的双手。“就是鲍勃，绝对没错！我确信能在这找到你，只要你还健在。是啊，是啊，是啊！——二十年确实很长。鲍勃，那家老餐馆早已不见，多希望它还在，那样我们就可以在这里再进晚餐。在西部干得咋样，老哥们？”

“没错！我要啥，它给啥。你变化很大，吉米。没想到你竟长高了两三英寸！”

“哦，我二十岁后又长了点儿。”

“在纽约混得不错吧，吉米？”

“还行！我在市政府的一个部门里上班。走吧，鲍勃，我知道一个地方，咱们去那儿好好聊聊我们的过去。”

二人挽着胳膊沿街往前走着。被成功冲昏了头脑的西部来客开始讲述自己的发迹史。而另一位则把头埋在大衣领子里，饶有兴趣地倾听着。

overcoat, listened with interest.

At the corner stood a drug store, brilliant with electric lights. When they came into this glare each of them turned simultaneously to gaze upon the other's face.

The man from the West stopped suddenly and released his arm.

"You're not Jimmy Wells," he snapped. "Twenty years is a long time, but not long enough to change a man's nose from a Roman to a pug."

"It sometimes changes a good man into a bad one," said the tall man. "You've been under arrest for ten minutes, 'Silky' Bob. Chicago thinks you may have dropped over our way and wires us she wants to have a chat with you. Going quietly, are you? That's sensible. Now, before we go on to the station here's a note I was asked to hand you. You may read it here at the window. It's from Patrolman Wells."

The man from the West unfolded the little piece of paper handed him. His hand was steady when he began to read, but it trembled a little by the time he had finished. The note was rather short.

Bob:

I was at the appointed place on time. When you struck the match to light your cigar I saw it was the face of the man wanted in Chicago. Somehow I couldn't do it myself, so I went around and got a plain clothes man to do the job.

JIMMY

拐角处是家药店，灯火明亮。二人来到灯光下，不约而同地都转过身目视对方的脸。

西部来客一下子停住脚步，松开了胳膊。

“你不是吉米·威尔斯！”他怒声道。“二十年是很长，但还不至于把一个人的罗马鼻变成塌塌鼻！”

“但却可能把一个好人变成坏人。”那高个男子反唇相讥。“十分钟前你就已经被捕了，‘滑头’鲍勃。芝加哥警方猜到你会窜到我们这儿，便拍电报给我们，说他们要跟你‘聊聊’。乖乖地跟我走如何？聪明点儿。去警局前先给你看个纸条，有人让我交给你。你可以在窗前看看，是威尔斯巡警给你的。”

那人打开了递到手里的小纸条。他的手开始还很沉稳，但看完后有点颤抖了。纸条很短：

鲍勃：

我如期到了约会地址。你划火柴点燃雪茄烟时，我看出，你的脸正是芝加哥警方通缉的那张脸。不知怎么，我下不了手，便找了一个便衣警察来干这活儿。

吉米

The Gift of the Magi
圣贤的礼物[①]

① 此处将英语原文标题中的"Magi"译成"圣贤",是借鉴了黄源深老师的译法(详见黄源深译:《最后一片叶子——欧·亨利短篇小说选》,上海译文出版社,2011年版第67页)。"Magi"是Magus的复数形式。依据基督教传统,"Magi"是指来自东方的三位贤人,给出生在马槽里的耶稣送来礼物,通常认为是世上第一份圣诞礼物。现有已出版的译文中,"Magi"通常音译成"麦琪",但这种译法有可能误导读者,以为文中有一个叫"麦琪"的人。

本篇讲述的是一个关于爱与奉献的故事。德拉和吉姆是一对小夫妻，生活贫寒却恩爱有加。他们家有两件宝贝，一件是德拉如瀑的长发，另一件是吉姆那块祖传的金表。圣诞节前一天，德拉希望能为她的丈夫买一件特别的礼物。但尽管她平日里精打细算、省吃俭用，总共也只积攒下来一美元八十七美分。无奈之下，纵有万般不舍，德拉还是决定卖掉她一头长长的秀发，为她丈夫买了一根精致的白金怀表短链。可是等到吉姆回到家，德拉却悲喜交加地发现：吉姆已卖掉他的金表，为她买回了渴慕已久的一套漂亮梳子。由于这样的阴差阳错，他们送给彼此的圣诞礼物暂时都用不上了，这不能不让人遗憾，但感人至深的却是他们彼此之间的深爱以及他们为了爱而甘愿付出一切的精神！爱——这份弥足珍贵的礼物，是他们送给彼此的最好的圣诞礼物！

One dollar and eighty-seven cents. That was all. And sixty cents of it was in pennies. Pennies saved one and two at a time by bulldozing the grocer and the vegetable man and the butcher until one's cheeks burned with the silent imputation of parsimony that such close dealing implied. Three times Della counted it. One dollar and eighty-seven cents. And the next day would be Christmas.

There was clearly nothing left to do but flop down on the shabby little couch and howl. So Della did it. Which instigates the moral reflection that life is made up of sobs, sniffles, and smiles, with sniffles predominating.

While the mistress of the home is gradually subsiding from the first stage to the second, take a look at the home. A furnished flat at $8 per week. It did not exactly beggar description①, but it certainly had that word on the look-out for the mendicancy② squad③.

In the vestibule④ below was a letter-box into which no letter would go, and an electric button from which no mortal finger could coax a ring. Also appertaining thereunto was a card bearing the name "Mr. James Dillingham Young."

The "Dillingham" had been flung to the breeze during a former period of prosperity when its possessor was being paid $30 per week. Now, when the income was shrunk to $20, the letters of "Dillingham" looked blurred, as though they were thinking seriously of contracting to a modest and unassuming

① beggar description 难以相信，无法形容 ② mendicancy *n.* 行乞
③ squad 警察队伍 ④ vestibule *n.* 前厅，门厅

一块八毛七。总共就这么点儿！其中有六毛都是钢镚儿。这还是她每次买东西时一点点儿省下来的，为此，每次她都得死皮赖脸地让杂货铺商贩、菜贩或者肉贩给她便宜一分两分的，直至最后，他们一个个不得不乖乖就范，但对她这个吝啬鬼的极度鄙视却明明白白地写在脸上了。的确，这让谁见了不替她感到脸红害臊呢。德拉反反复复数了三遍，还是一块八毛七。而第二天就是圣诞节了。

她无可奈何，只好趴到小小的破旧的长沙发上失声痛哭。德拉只能这样呀。这场景不由得让人心生感慨，原来生活中有呜咽、抽泣和微笑，而抽泣是生活的常态。

屋内的女主人逐渐从呜咽转为抽泣，我们来看看她的屋子吧。这是一套带家具的公寓，每周的租金是八美元。虽然并非破旧得完全难以形容，但可用的词语定会引来负责逮捕街上流浪汉的警察的注意。

楼下门厅里有一个信箱，但从未有信件放进去。还有一个电子按钮，但从未有凡人的手指去按响它。旁边还贴着一张名片，上面写着詹姆斯·迪林厄姆·杨先生。

以前名片的主人每周能挣三十美元，日子过得还算宽裕，一时兴起便在姓和名之间添加了“迪林厄姆”。但如今每周收入缩减为二十美元，“Dillingham”几个字母看起来已模糊不清，它们似乎认真地考虑要收缩为一个不起眼、不张扬的 D（迪）呢。不过不管

D. But whenever Mr. James Dillingham Young came home and reached his flat above he was called "Jim" and greatly hugged by Mrs. James Dillingham Young, already introduced to you as Della, which is all very good.

Della finished her cry and attended to her cheeks with the powder rag. She stood by the window and looked out dully at a grey cat walking a grey fence in a grey backyard. Tomorrow would be Christmas Day, and she had only $1.87 with which to buy Jim a present. She had been saving every penny she could for months, with this result. Twenty dollars a week doesn't go far. Expenses had been greater than she had calculated. They always are. Only $1.87 to buy a present for Jim. Her Jim. Many a happy hour she had spent planning for something nice for him. Something fine and rare and sterling—something just a little bit near to being worthy of the honor of being owned by Jim.

There was a pier-glass between the windows of the room. Perhaps you have seen a pier-glass in an $8 flat. A very thin and very agile person may, by observing his reflection in a rapid sequence of longitudinal strips, obtain a fairly accurate conception of his looks. Della, being slender, had mastered the art.

Suddenly she whirled from the window and stood before the glass. Her eyes were shining brilliantly, but her face had lost its color within twenty seconds. Rapidly she pulled down her hair and let it fall to its full length.

Now, there were two possessions of the James Dillingham Youngs in which they both took a mighty pride. One was Jim's gold watch that had been his father's and his grandfather's. The

詹姆斯·迪林厄姆·杨先生什么时候回家，只要走到楼上的房间，詹姆斯·迪林厄姆·杨夫人，也就是前面介绍过的德拉，就会热烈地拥抱他，亲昵地称呼他为“吉姆”，一切看起来都挺好。

德拉停止了哭泣，用粉扑擦了擦面颊。她站到窗前，无精打采地看着窗外一只灰猫在灰色后院沿着灰色篱笆散步。明天就是圣诞节了，她只有一块八毛七，只有这点钱给吉姆买礼物。她攒了好几个月的钱，能省就省，才积攒下这么点儿。每周二十块完全不够花。各项开销总是比她估算得要多，向来如此。只有一块八毛七可用来为她亲爱的吉姆买一份礼物。德拉老早就开始盘算给吉姆买什么礼物了，而且每次一想起来就觉得幸福满满。买给他的礼物得很好、得稀有、还得质量上乘——大抵配得上他才行。

屋里的两扇窗户之间，有一面穿衣镜。你可能曾见过房租八美元的公寓里那样的穿衣镜吧。[①]一位身材瘦削、动作敏捷之人，也许可以通过观察镜子里反射出的一连串的长条影像，对自身相貌有个大致不差的概念。身材苗条的德拉对此倒是精通。

德拉突然从窗前转过身，站到镜子前。两只眼睛里闪烁着明亮的光芒，但二十秒之内，她的面容却黯然失色。她迅速披散开头发，让一头秀发倾泻而下。

詹姆斯·迪林厄姆·杨家拥有两件让他们都引以为豪的宝贝。

① 这种穿衣镜并不是由整块玻璃制成，而是由若干块狭长的玻璃拼凑而成，因此价格便宜，但这种镜子却很难让一个人看清自己的全貌。不过德拉掌握了照这种镜子的技巧。这里英文用的是 pier-glass。

other was Della's hair. Had the Queen of Sheba lived in the flat across the airshaft[①], Della would have let her hair hang out of the window some day to dry just to depreciate[②] Her Majesty's jewels and gifts. Had King Solomon been the janitor[③], with all his treasures piled up in the basement, Jim would have pulled out his watch every time he passed, just to see him pluck[④] at his beard from envy.

So now Della's beautiful hair fell about her, rippling and shining like a cascade of brown waters. It reached below her knee and made itself almost a garment for her. And then she did it up again nervously and quickly. Once she faltered[⑤] for a minute and stood still while a tear or two splashed on the worn red carpet.

On went her old brown jacket; on went her old brown hat. With a whirl of skirts and with the brilliant sparkle still in her eyes, she cluttered out of the door and down the stairs to the street.

Where she stopped the sign read: "Mme Sofronie. Hair Goods of All Kinds." One flight up Della ran, and collected herself, panting. Madame, large, too white, chilly, hardly looked the "Sofronie."

"Will you buy my hair?" asked Della.

"I buy hair," said Madame. "Take yer hat off and let's have a sight at the looks of it."

---

① airshaft *n.* 通风井 ② depreciate *v.* 贬低，轻视 ③ janitor *n.* 看门人
④ pluck *v.* 摘，拔 ⑤ falter *v.* 犹豫，畏缩

一件是吉姆的金表，那是从他的祖父、父亲那里一辈辈传下来的。另一件就是德拉的头发。如果示巴女王[1]就住在通风口对面的公寓，德拉某天一定会把她的长发垂于窗外晾干，只为了让女王陛下的珠宝与礼物相形见绌。如果所罗门王[2]把所有的金银珠宝都堆放于地下室，并且亲自把门，吉姆每次路过时也会取出手表，仅仅为了让所罗门王嫉妒得不停地拉扯胡子。

此时此刻，德拉美丽的头发披散在她全身，像棕色的水瀑呈波状起伏，熠熠闪光。这过膝的长发，看起来就像她的一件外衣。紧接着，她神经质地迅速扎起头发。她迟疑了片刻，而后一动不动地站立着，这时一两颗泪珠溅落到破旧的红地毯上。

穿上褐色的旧外套，戴上褐色的旧帽子。虽然仍泪光闪闪，德拉长裙一旋，夺门而出，下了楼，来到大街上。

在一个写着“法国索芙朗妮夫人头发制品商店”的牌子前，德拉停下了脚步。她跨上一级台阶，让心情平复下来，不过仍气喘吁吁。映入眼帘的女店主体形魁梧、面色苍白、表情冷漠，压根儿看不出“法国索芙朗妮夫人”的样子。[3]

“你愿意买我的头发吗？”德拉问。

“我买头发，”女店主回答，“摘下你的帽子，让我看下啥样。”

---

① 示巴女王 Queen of Sheba，取材自《圣经·旧约》的“列王记”。传说中的示巴女王惊艳绝伦，是古代阿拉伯半岛赛伯伊王国的女王。遇见所罗门王之后，十分爱慕其英明及刚毅，两人有过一段甜蜜恋情。

② 所罗门王 King Solomon，是犹太民族历史上最伟大的君王。据《圣经》记载，所罗门王在20岁登基后，曾在梦中向上帝祈求智慧。上帝不仅赐给他无与伦比的智慧，还赐给他无尽的荣耀、财富以及美德。

③ 在欧·亨利的时代，美国买卖及经营头发用品的商店多追随法国风尚，所以店名多取法国名。但德拉眼里的店老板看起来并不像典型的法国女人，所以该店多半是个冒牌法国店。

Down rippled the brown cascade.

"Twenty dollars," said Madame, lifting the mass with a practised hand.

"Give it to me quick," said Della.

Oh, and the next two hours tripped by on rosy wings. Forget the hashed metaphor. She was ransacking[①] the stores for Jim's present.

She found it at last. It surely had been made for Jim and no one else. There was no other like it in any of the stores, and she had turned all of them inside out. It was a platinum fob chain simple and chaste in design, properly proclaiming its value by substance alone and not by meretricious[②] ornamentation—as all good things should do. It was even worthy of The Watch. As soon as she saw it she knew that it must be Jim's. It was like him. Quietness and value—the description applied to both. Twenty-one dollars they took from her for it, and she hurried home with the 87 cents. With that chain on his watch Jim might be properly anxious about the time in any company. Grand as the watch was, he sometimes looked at it on the sly on account of the old leather strap that he used in place of a chain.

When Della reached home her intoxication[③] gave way a little to prudence and reason. She got out her curling irons and lighted the gas and went to work repairing the ravages[④] made by generosity added to love. Which is always a tremendous task dear friends—a mammoth task.

---

① ransack v. 翻遍 ② meretricious *adj.* 华而不实的

③ intoxication *n.* 陶醉 ④ ravage *n.* 灾害，破坏

瀑布般棕色的头发呈波状倾泻而下。

“二十块。”女店主说着，用训练有素的手拧起一团头发。

“快给我。”德拉说道。

接下来的两小时就像长了玫瑰色的翅膀似的飞掠而过。不过别在意这个糟糕透顶的比喻。总之，德拉为了给吉姆搜寻合适的礼物，逛了一家又一家商店。

她终于找到了。那简直就是专为吉姆准备的，非他莫属。而且其他店里都没有，她已经把其他店里的都看了个底朝天。这是一个白金的怀表短链，样式简洁大方，只要凭材质就能看出品质不凡，无需其他任何烦琐的装饰——所有的好东西均如此。这个表链与那块金表刚好般配。德拉一眼望过去，就觉得它就应该是吉姆的。物如其人。沉着冷静而富有内涵——这个形容吉姆和表链都恰如其分。他们把表链二十一块钱卖给了她，她匆匆回到家，身上只剩下八毛七。有那根表链搭配吉姆的金表，以后在任何场合他都可以大大方方地看时间了。虽然金表看来大气庄重，但是他时常只能偷偷地瞄一眼，因为本应装上表链的地方现在却是一根破旧的皮带子。

德拉回到家，兴奋之情渐渐褪去，逐渐变得谨慎和理智。她拿出卷发棒，点燃煤气炉[①]，开始修复她那出于爱之慷慨而彻底毁掉的头发。爱总是一项极大的任务，亲爱的朋友——甚至是艰巨的任务。

① 如今的卷发棒都是用电，而欧·亨利的时代主要用煤气，所以使用卷发棒之前先得在煤气炉上烤热。

Within forty minutes her head was covered with tiny, close-lying curls that made her look wonderfully like a truant[①] schoolboy. She looked at her reflection in the mirror long, carefully, and critically.

"If Jim doesn't kill me," she said to herself, "before he takes a second look at me, he'll say I look like a Coney Island chorus girl. But what could I do—oh! What could I do with a dollar and eighty-seven cents?"

At 7 o'clock the coffee was made and the frying-pan was on the back of the stove hot and ready to cook the chops.

Jim was never late. Della doubled the fob chain in her hand and sat on the corner of the table near the door that he always entered. Then she heard his step on the stair away down on the first flight, and she turned white for just a moment. She had a habit of saying little silent prayers about the simplest everyday things, and now she whispered: "Please, God, make him think I am still pretty."

The door opened and Jim stepped in and closed it. He looked thin and very serious. Poor fellow, he was only twenty-two—and to be burdened with a family! He needed a new overcoat and he was without gloves.

Jim stepped inside the door, as immovable as a setter at the scent of quail[②]. His eyes were fixed upon Della, and there was an expression in them that she could not read, and it terrified her. It was not anger, nor surprise, nor disapproval, nor horror, nor any of the sentiments that she had been prepared for. He simply

① truant *adj.* 逃学的 ② quail *n.* 鹌鹑

不到四十分钟，德拉已是满头服服帖帖的小发卷了，像极了一个逃学的小男孩。她用专注而挑剔的目光，长久地看着镜子里的自己。

“即使第一眼见了我不杀我，”她自言自语道，“在他看我第二眼之前，他肯定会说我像康尼岛[①]上唱合唱的女孩。但是我能咋办呢？唉！一块八毛七能买什么呢？”

晚上七点，咖啡煮好了，煎锅已在炉子上加热，随时都可以煎肉排。

吉姆从来不会晚回家。德拉把怀表短链对折握在手里，坐在桌子靠门的一角。吉姆总是从那里走进门。这时，她远远地听见他上楼的脚步声，脸色瞬间煞白。德拉有个习惯，对于最简单的日常说事，她都会在心里默默祈祷，此刻她轻声低语道：“恳求我的上帝！让他觉得我依然好看吧！”

门打开了，吉姆走进来，随手关上了门。他看起来身材消瘦，神情肃穆。可怜的小伙子！ 他才二十二岁——却已背负养家糊口的重担。他需要一件新大衣，也缺一双手套。

吉姆走进屋，像塞特种猎犬闻到了鹌鹑气味似的一动不动。他的眼睛注视着德拉，有一种她读不懂的神情，让她感到害怕。不是生气，不是惊讶，不是厌恶，也不是恐惧，反正不是她预料中的任何一种情绪反应。他只是一动不动地注视着她，脸上呈现出一种异样的神情。

① 康尼岛，Coney Island，是位于美国纽约市布鲁克林区的半岛，20世纪初成为纽约知名的休闲娱乐区域。

stared at her fixedly with that peculiar expression on his face.

Della wriggled off the table and went for him.

"Jim, darling," she cried, "don't look at me that way. I had my hair cut off and sold it because I couldn't have lived through Christmas without giving you a present. It'll grow out again—you won't mind, will you? I just had to do it. My hair grows awfully fast. Say 'Merry Christmas!' Jim, and let's be happy. You don't know what a nice—what a beautiful, nice gift I've got for you."

"You've cut off your hair?" asked Jim, laboriously①, as if he had not arrived at that patent fact yet, even after the hardest mental labor.

"Cut it off and sold it," said Della. "Don't you like me just as well, anyhow? I'm me without my hair, ain't I?"

Jim looked about the room curiously.

"You say your hair is gone?" he said, with an air almost of idiocy.

"You needn't look for it," said Della. "It's sold, I tell you—sold and gone, too. It's Christmas Eve, boy. Be good to me, for it went for you. Maybe the hairs of my head were numbered," she went on with a sudden serious sweetness, "but nobody could ever count my love for you. Shall I put the chops on, Jim?"

Out of his trance Jim seemed quickly to wake. He enfolded his Della. For ten seconds let us regard with discreet② scrutiny some inconsequential③ object in the other direction. Eight

① laboriously *adv.* 艰苦地 ② discreet *adj.* 谨慎的
③ inconsequential *adj.* 微不足道的

德拉好不容易从桌子边站起来，向他走去。

"吉姆，亲爱的，"她哭了起来，"不要这样看着我呀。我把头发剪了卖掉了，是因为如果圣诞节不送给你一份礼物，我是无法安心度过的。头发会再长起来的——你不会介意的，对吧？我只能剪掉它了。我的头发长得超快的。说'圣诞快乐！'吉姆，我们高兴一下吧。你不知道我给你买了一件多么好——多么漂亮、多么好看的礼物。"

"你把头发剪掉了？"吉姆问，仿佛是在绞尽脑汁之后，仍然没能认清眼前显而易见的事实。

"剪掉卖了。"德拉说，"你仍然喜欢我，对吧？长发没了，但我依然是我，对不对？"

吉姆急切地环顾屋子四周。

"你说你的头发没了？"他说着，神态近乎白痴。

"你不用找了。"德拉说。"已经卖了，我告诉你——卖了就没了。今天是平安夜，我心爱的人儿！你得对我好，因为我是为了你才卖掉我的头发的。也许我的头发有多少根可以数得清，"她突然一脸认真地、甜甜地说道，"但是我对你的爱没有任何人可以数得清的。①我可以把肉排放进锅了吗，吉姆？"

吉姆似乎猛然清醒。他抱住了心爱的德拉。花十秒钟的时间，让我们审慎地观察下屋内其他方向的一些不相干之物。②一周八美

① 《圣经》里说："Our days are numbered"（我们的日子是数得清的），正如此处提到的"也许我们头上的头发是数得清的（Maybe the hairs of my head were numbered）"。隐含意义是每个人终将离开人世，没有人可以永生。

② 这里叙述者的言外之意是，因为两个小夫妻在拥抱，我们读者还是不要盯着他们看，最好将视线转移到屋子里的其他地方。

dollars a week or a million a year—what is the difference? A mathematician or a wit would give you the wrong answer. The magi brought valuable gifts, but that was not among them. This dark assertion will be illuminated later on.

Jim drew a package from his overcoat pocket and threw it upon the table.

"Don't make any mistake, Della," he said, "about me. I don't think there's anything in the way of a haircut or a shave or a shampoo that could make me like my girl any less. But if you'll unwrap that package you may see why you had me going awhile at first."

White fingers and nimble tore at the string and paper. And then an ecstatic scream of joy; and then, alas! A quick feminine change to hysterical tears and wails, necessitating[①] the immediate employment of all the comforting powers of the lord of the flat.

For there lay The Combs—the set of combs, side and back, that Della had worshipped for long in a Broadway window. Beautiful combs, pure tortoise-shell, with jewelled rims—just the shade to wear in the beautiful vanished hair. They were expensive combs, she knew, and her heart had simply craved and yearned over them without the least hope of possession. And now, they were hers, but the tresses that should have adorned the coveted[②] adornments were gone.

But she hugged them to her bosom, and at length she was able to look up with dim eyes and a smile and say: "My hair

① necessitate *v.* 使成为必要 ② covet *v.* 垂涎

元和一年一百万美元——有什么区别？数学家和诙谐风趣之人给你的都是错误答案。来自东方的三位贤人带来了珍贵的礼物，但是他们并没有带来答案。这句话听起来晦涩，但其意思稍后将不言自明。

吉姆从大衣口袋里拿出一包东西，扔到桌上。

“不要做错事，德拉，”他说，“不要因为我做错事。在我看来，剪什么样的发型，是否刮汗毛，用什么牌子的洗发水，这些都不会削弱我对心爱人儿的爱。但是你打开那包东西，就会明白我先前为什么会是那副模样了。”

德拉用白净而灵巧的手指拆开包扎的绳子和纸。先是欣喜若狂，紧接着发出一声叹息，“哎呀！”很快变成女人歇斯底里般的泪奔和号啕，需要这间屋子的男主人使出浑身解数来安抚。

里面包裹的是一套发梳——两鬓用的、后脑用的，一应俱全。这套梳子德拉曾在百老汇大街的一个橱窗里见过，从此心驰神往。纯正的玳瑁制成的美梳，边上还镶嵌有珠宝——色泽正好配得上原有的秀发。德拉知道这套梳子特别昂贵，原本只是心向往之，但从来不曾奢求占有。如今，这套梳子归她所有，但能使她渴望已久的美梳生色的披肩长发却没有了。

德拉把梳子捧到胸前，泪眼模糊地抬头看着吉姆，微笑着说：“我的头发长得很快的，吉姆！”

grows so fast, Jim!"

And then Della leaped up like a little singed cat and cried, "Oh, oh!"

Jim had not yet seen his beautiful present. She held it out to him eagerly upon her open palm. The dull precious metal seemed to flash with a reflection of her bright and ardent spirit.

"Isn't it a dandy, Jim? I hunted all over town to find it. You'll have to look at the time a hundred times a day now. Give me your watch. I want to see how it looks on it."

Instead of obeying, Jim tumbled down on the couch and put his hands under the back of his head and smiled.

"Dell," said he, "let's put our Christmas presents away and keep 'em awhile①. They're too nice to use just at present. I sold the watch to get the money to buy your combs. And now suppose you put the chops on."

The magi, as you know, were wise men—wonderfully wise men—who brought gifts to the Babe in the manger. They invented the art of giving Christmas presents. Being wise, their gifts were no doubt wise ones, possibly bearing the privilege of exchange in case of duplication. And here I have lamely related to you the uneventful②chronicle of two foolish children in a flat who most unwisely sacrificed for each other the greatest treasures of their house. But in a last word to the wise of these days let it be said that of all who give gifts these two were the wisest. Of all who give and receive gifts, such as they are wisest. Everywhere they are wisest. They are the Magi.

① awhile adv. 片刻，一会儿 ② uneventful adj. 平淡无奇的

就在这时，德拉像只被烧焦的小猫一样跳了起来，大声叫喊："啊呀，啊呀！"

吉姆还没有看到送给他的漂亮礼物呢。她摊开手掌，急切地递给他看。色彩本不明亮的贵金属，似乎随着她灿烂而真诚的表情显得熠熠生辉。

"是不是极好，吉姆？我跑遍了整个小镇才找到的。你现在一天看一百次时间都没问题。把你的金表给我。我想看看配上这个表链的样子。"

吉姆没有听从，而是一下子倒在长沙发上，用双手枕着头，面露微笑。

"德拉，"他说，"我们把圣诞礼物都放到一边，先保存起来吧。它们太好看了，现在用太可惜了。我把金表卖了，给你买了梳子。现在可以把肉排放进锅里了。"

如你们所知，三贤人都是智者——极富智慧之人——他们给马槽里初生的耶稣带来了礼物。他们发明了送圣诞礼物的艺术。他们是智者，所以他们赠送的礼物必然是充满智慧的选择，纵然是一模一样的，仍有交换的价值。这里我讲述的是发生在一套公寓里的两个傻孩子身上的平凡故事，他们为了彼此，不明智地牺牲了家里最珍贵的两件宝贝。但是最后，我想对当今社会的聪明人说，在所有赠送礼物的人当中，他们是最聪明的。在所有互赠礼物的人当中，如他们这般的人是最聪明的。在任何地方，他们都是最聪明的。他们就是贤人。

Roads of Destiny
命运之路

命运究竟能不能由自己掌控？这是本篇故事重点探讨的问题。而答案是否定的。故事的主人公是一位牧羊少年，他一心想成为诗人。当站在命运的三岔路口时，他进行了三种命运的预设，最终结果却都是死于侯爵的枪之下，可谓殊途同归。欧·亨利就是用这样一种三重命运并置的方式，描绘了一个小人物的悲剧。牧羊少年无论选择什么道路，结局都不会有任何改观，他最终死于不切实际的诗人梦，从最开始的囿于幻想、沉迷女色，到最后的诗人梦幻灭，让我们见证了他性格中的多重弱点。读完这篇小说，我们不禁为牧羊少年的悲惨结局叹息，为牧羊少年未能圆梦而叹息，但同时也明白了一个道理：播种一种性格，收获一种命运。你的未来取决于你本质上是个什么样的人，而偶然的选择并无法书写我们的命运。

I go to seek on many roads What is to be.
True heart and strong, with love to light—
Will they not bear me in the fight
To order, shun or wield or mould
My Destiny?

Unpublished Poems of David Mignot

The song was over. The words were David's; the air, one of the countryside. The company about the inn table applauded heartily, for the young poet paid for the wine. Only the notary, M. Papineau, shook his head a little at the lines, for he was a man of books, and he had not drunk with the rest.

David went out into the village street, where the night air drove the wine vapor from his head. And then he remembered that he and Yvonne had quarreled that day, and that he had resolved to leave his home that night to seek fame and honor in the great world outside.

"When my poems are on every man's tongue," he told himself, in a fine exhilaration, "she will, perhaps, think of the hard words she spoke this day."

Except the roisterers in the tavern, the village folk were abed. David crept softly into his room in the shed of his father's cottage and made a bundle of his small store of clothing. With this upon a staff, he set his face outward upon the road that ran from Vernoy.

He passed his father's herd of sheep, huddled in their nightly pen—the sheep he herded daily, leaving them to scatter

我在多条路上苦苦寻觅人生的意蕴
情真意切，爱情照明——
难道这些不足以支撑我在战斗中
主宰、回避、左右或铸就
我的命运？

大卫·米格诺特尚未问世的诗

曲终。歌词出自大卫之手，曲调具有乡村气息。一群人围坐在小酒馆的一张桌子旁热烈鼓掌，因为那位年轻的诗人给他们付了酒钱。只有公证人帕皮诺听了歌词后摇摇头，作为一个读书人，他是不会和那帮人一起饮酒作乐的。

大卫出了小酒馆，来到乡村大街上，夜晚的空气驱散了他的醉意。就在这时，他记起那天和伊冯娜吵了一架，当晚即决定离家出走，去大千世界追寻功成名就。

“当我写的诗歌人人传诵时，”他忘乎所以地自言自语道，“她或许会后悔今天说过的狠话。”

除了酒馆里还在吵闹的醉汉，村民们都已进入梦乡。大卫轻手轻脚地进了自己的屋，一间搭在父亲房子旁的棚屋而已。收拾完衣服，打成小包。他找了根棍子挑着，便往外走去，踏上离开维诺伊的大道。

他经过父亲的羊圈，夜晚羊群都蜷缩在一起——这群他每天放牧的羊，不过一旦他写起诗来，羊群便到处乱跑。此时，伊冯娜的房

while he wrote verses on scraps of paper. He saw a light yet shining in Yvonne's window, and a weakness shook his purpose of a sudden. Perhaps that light meant that she rued, sleepless, her anger, and that morning might—But, no! His decision was made. Vernoy was no place for him. Not one soul there could share his thoughts. Out along that road lay his fate and his future.

Three leagues across the dim, moonlit champaign ran the road, straight as a ploughman's furrow. It was believed in the village that the road ran to Paris, at least; and this name the poet whispered often to himself as he walked. Never so far from Vernoy had David travelled before.

THE LEFT BRANCH

Three leagues, then, the road ran, and turned into a puzzle. It joined with another and a larger road at right angles. David stood, uncertain, for a while, and then took the road to the left.

Upon this more important highway were, imprinted in the dust, wheel tracks left by the recent passage of some vehicle. Some half an hour later these traces were verified by the sight of a ponderous carriage mired in a little brook at the bottom of a steep hill. The driver and postilions were shouting and tugging at the horses' bridles. On the road at one side stood a huge, black-clothed man and a slender lady wrapped in a long, light cloak.

David saw the lack of skill in the efforts of the servants. He quietly assumed control of the work. He directed the outriders to cease their clamor at the horses and to exercise their strength upon

间里还亮着灯，让他突然心头一软。也许这道光表明她懊悔自己发了火而难以入眠，也许到了早晨就——但是，不！他去意已定。维诺伊已没有他的容身之地。在这儿没人能听他倾诉衷肠。而路的前方才是他命运的归宿。

穿过月光下昏暗的原野，这条路笔直如犁沟，足足有三里格[①]长。村民们都相信，至少这条路能通往巴黎。诗人时不时地边走边念叨这个地名。大卫平生第一次走出维诺伊这么远。

左岔路

道路不断向前延伸，至三里格之外，已逐渐让人辨不清方向。这条道与另一条更宽的路垂直相交。大卫站在那儿，举棋不定，过了一会儿，决定沿左边那条道继续往前走。

在这条更为重要的康庄大道上，脚下的尘土上留有几条刚刚碾过的车轮印痕。大约过了半小时，他发现前面一辆笨重马车陷进了陡峭的小山脚下的小溪里，动弹不得；这些印痕就是这辆马车留下的。车夫和左马驭手正一边拽着马的缰绳，一边大声吆喝。在路的另一边，站着一位身材魁梧的黑衣男子和一位身披浅色长披风的苗条女子。

大卫看到那些仆人虽然很用力，但却明显不得法。他不声不响地走过去帮忙。他指挥马车侍从停止对马大喊大叫，把力气用在推车轮上。让车夫一个人用他熟悉的声音鞭策马儿；大卫则用自己强

① leagues，里格〔旧时长度单位，相当于3英里或3海里〕。

the wheels. The driver alone urged the animals with his familiar voice; David himself heaved a powerful shoulder at the rear of the carriage, and with one harmonious tug the great vehicle rolled up on solid ground. The outriders climbed to their places.

David stood for a moment upon one foot. The huge gentleman waved a hand. "You will enter the carriage," he said, in a voice large, like himself, but smoothed by art and habit. Obedience belonged in the path of such a voice. Brief as was the young poet's hesitation, it was cut shorter still by a renewal of the command. David's foot went to the step. In the darkness he perceived dimly the form of the lady upon the rear seat. He was about to seat himself opposite, when the voice again swayed him to its will. "You will sit at the lady's side."

The gentleman swung his great weight to the forward seat. The carriage proceeded up the hill. The lady was shrunk, silent, into her corner. David could not estimate whether she was old or young, but a delicate, mild perfume from her clothes stirred his poet's fancy to the belief that there was loveliness beneath the mystery. Here was an adventure such as he had often imagined. But as yet he held no key to it, for no word was spoken while he sat with his impenetrable companions.

In an hour's time David perceived through the window that the vehicle traversed the street of some town. Then it stopped in front of a closed and darkened house, and a postilion alighted to hammer impatiently upon the door. A latticed window above flew wide and a night capped head popped out.

"Who are ye that disturb honest folk at this time of night?

有力的肩膀推马车后部。在大家的齐心协力下，这辆大车终于重新回到了坚实的路面上。马车侍从们也回到了原来的位置。

大卫单腿站立了一会儿。那位身材魁梧的先生朝他挥了挥手。“你到车上来吧。”他说，洪亮的嗓音正与他的体格相符，不过因为注意说话技巧和习惯，声音听起来倒也柔和。听到这种声音似乎唯有顺从。年轻诗人犹豫的刹那，命令再次响起。大卫爬上马车。黑暗中，他隐约看见后座那位女士的身姿。他正准备坐到对面，那个声音再次发出指令，“你坐到那位女士旁边。”

那个大块头男子拖着沉重的身体坐到前座。马车继续沿山路上行。那位女士蜷缩在角落里，一言不发。大卫看不出她多大年龄，但她衣服上散发出的一种淡雅的香味激发了这位诗人的想象。他觉得在神秘的面纱下，定有可人之处。这正是他以前常幻想的奇遇。不过他现在还心里没底，因为和他同车的两个人高深莫测，还未曾说过一句话。

一个小时过去了，大卫透过车窗发现马车驰骋在某个小镇的街道上。然后，马车停在一栋房门紧闭、黑不溜秋的屋子前，一个左马驭者上前不耐烦地锤起门来。上面的格子窗突然打开，钻出一个戴着睡帽的脑袋。

“这么晚了，是谁瞎敲门打扰我们这些老实人的？我的店已经

My house is closed. It's too late for profitable travelers to be abroad. Cease knocking at my door, and be off."

"Open!" spluttered the postilion, loudly; "open for Monsiegneur the Marquis de Beaupertuys."

"Ah!" cried the voice above. "Ten thousand pardons, my lord. I did not know—the hour is so late—at once shall the door be opened, and the house placed at my lord's disposal."

Inside was heard the clink of chain and bar, and the door was flung open. Shivering with chill and apprehension, the landlord of the Silver Flagon stood, half clad, candle in hand, upon the threshold.

David followed the Marquis out of the carriage. "Assist the lady," he was ordered. The poet obeyed. He felt her small hand tremble as he guided her descent. "Into the house," was the next command.

The room was the long dining-hall of the tavern. A great oak table ran down its length. The huge gentleman seated himself in a chair at the nearer end. The lady sank into another against the wall, with an air of great weariness. David stood, considering how best he might now take his leave and continue upon his way.

"My lord," said the landlord, bowing to the floor, "h-had I ex-expected this honor, entertainment would have been ready. T-t-there is wine and cold fowl and m-m-maybe—"

"Candles," said the marquis, spreading the fingers of one plump white hand in a gesture he had.

"Y-yes, my lord." He fetched half a dozen candles, lighted

关门，这么晚了，再有钱我也不会留宿了。别敲了，赶紧走吧！”

“开门！”侍从气急败坏地大声嚷道，“为博贝尔杜依侯爵开门。”

“啊！”楼上有声音大叫。“求您千万恕罪，大人。我有眼不识泰山——都这么晚了——门马上就开，房子大人随便住。”

里面传来链条和门闩的叮当声，门被猛地一下拉开。那银壶客栈的店主，衣服也没来得及穿好，手里拿着蜡烛，站在门槛上，在寒风中瑟瑟发抖。

大卫跟着侯爵走下马车。“扶一下小姐。”侯爵命令道。诗人听从。扶她下车时，他感觉到她的小手在颤抖。“进屋，”又是一道命令传来。

这是客栈里长长的餐厅。一张大橡木餐桌摆在那里。大块头先生坐在近处的椅子上，那位小姐倒在靠墙的一把椅子上，满脸倦容。大卫站在那里，考虑他该如何巧妙地告辞之后继续赶路。

“大人，”店主说道，一个深鞠躬都挨着地了，“如——如果在下知——知道您大驾光临，一定会提前做好迎接准备。这——这里还有一些酒和冷肉，可能——”

“蜡烛。”侯爵说着，张开白白胖胖的手指头，做了一个他特有的手势。

“好……好的，大人。”他拿来半打蜡烛，点燃后放在桌上。

them, and set them upon the table.

"If monsieur would, perhaps, deign to taste a certain Burgundy—there is a cask—"

"Candles," said monsieur, spreading his fingers.

"Assuredly—quickly—I fly, my lord."

A dozen more lighted candles shone in the hall. The great bulk of the marquis overflowed his chair. He was dressed in fine black from head to foot save for the snowy ruffles at his wrist and throat. Even the hilt and scabbard of his sword were black. His expression was one of sneering pride. The ends of an upturned moustache reached nearly to his mocking eyes.

The lady sat motionless, and now David perceived that she was young, and possessed of pathetic and appealing beauty. He was startled from the contemplation of her forlorn loveliness by the booming voice of the marquis.

"What is your name and pursuit?"

"David Mignot. I am a poet."

The moustache of the marquis curled nearer to his eyes.

"How do you live?"

"I am also a shepherd; I guarded my father's flock," David answered, with his head high, but a flush upon his cheek.

"Then listen, master shepherd and poet, to the fortune you have blundered upon tonight. This lady is my niece, Mademoiselle Lucie de Varennes. She is of noble descent and is possessed of ten thousand francs a year in her own right. As to her charms, you have but to observe for yourself. If the

"如果大人愿意赏脸品尝一下勃艮第葡萄酒[1]，还有一桶——"

"蜡烛。"先生伸出手指说。

"好的——马上就去——大人。"

大厅里又点了十几只蜡烛。侯爵坐的椅子还容不下他那庞大的身躯。他全身一袭黑色，只有袖口和衣领处的褶边是雪白的。甚至连剑柄和剑鞘都是黑色的。他充满高傲的表情里夹带着几分讥讽。八字胡高高上翘，两端几乎碰到他那双充满嘲弄的眼睛。

那位小姐一动不动地坐着，这时大卫才发现她其实很年轻，面容姣好，楚楚动人。正当他沉浸于那冷艳的容颜之中，侯爵的低沉有力的声音震醒了他。

"你叫什么名字？是干什么的？"

"大卫·米格诺特，我是一位诗人。"

侯爵的胡子翘起来，离眼睛更近了。

"你靠什么谋生？"

"我还是一个牧羊人，帮我父亲看护羊群。"大卫抬起头回答道，但是不免面露羞愧之情。

"那么听着，会写诗的牧羊人，今晚你是走了大运了。这位小姐是我的侄女，露西·德瓦雷斯小姐。她出身尊贵，收入不菲，年入一万法郎。至于她的美貌，只有你自己亲眼看了。如果这些条件能够让你这个牧羊人心动的话，只要你一句话，她便能嫁你为妻。别

① 勃艮第葡萄酒（Burgundy）：产于法国勃艮第地区的葡萄酒统称，被誉为"法国葡萄酒之王"。

inventory pleases your shepherd's heart, she becomes your wife at a word. Do not interrupt me. Tonight I conveyed her to the chateau of the Comte de Villemaur, to whom her hand had been promised. Guests were present; the priest was waiting; her marriage to one eligible in rank and fortune was ready to be accomplished. At the altar this demoiselle, so meek and dutiful, turned upon me like a leopardess, charged me with cruelty and crimes, and broke, before the gaping priest, the troth I had plighted for her. I swore there and then, by ten thousand devils, that she should marry the first man we met after leaving the chateau, be he prince, charcoal-burner, or thief. You, shepherd, are the first. Mademoiselle must be wed this night. If not you, then another. You have ten minutes in which to make your decision. Do not vex me with words or questions. Ten minutes, shepherd; and they are speeding."

The marquis drummed loudly with his white fingers upon the table. He sank into a veiled attitude of waiting. It was as if some great house had shut its doors and windows against approach. David would have spoken, but the huge man's bearing stopped his tongue. Instead, he stood by the lady's chair and bowed.

"Mademoiselle," he said, and he marveled to find his words flowing easily before so much elegance and beauty. "You have heard me say I was a shepherd. I have also had the fancy, at times, that I am a poet. If it be the test of a poet to adore and cherish the beautiful, that fancy is now strengthened. Can I serve you in any way, mademoiselle?"

打断我。今晚我本来带她去孔德维尔莫城堡完婚的。客人和神父都在场等候。她本要与一个门当户对的人完婚。可到了圣坛前，这个平日里温文尔雅、百依百顺的小姐，竟像一只母豹一样朝我扑过来，骂我残酷无情，罪大恶极，弄得神父目瞪口呆，就这样毁了这桩婚约。我当场对天发誓，必须把她嫁给我们离开城堡后遇见的第一个男人，无论他是王子、烧煤人还是小偷。而你，牧羊人，就是我们所遇见的第一个男人。小姐今晚必须结婚。不是你，就是其他人。你有十分钟的时间来做出决定。别说话，也别问我任何问题，否则会惹恼我。就十分钟，牧羊人，时间可不等人哦。”

侯爵白皙的手指把桌子敲得咚咚直响。然后他开始面无表情地等待。仿佛一座大厦门窗紧闭，让人难以靠近。大卫本来想说些什么，可那位大块头的态度令他语塞。因此，他站到小姐的椅子旁，对她深深地鞠了一躬。

“小姐，”他说道，并且惊叹自己在如此美丽的女子面前竟然还能坐怀不乱地讲出话来，“你知道我是个牧羊人，有时我也幻想自己是一名诗人。如果诗人得接受爱美惜美的考验，那么现在这个幻想就更加强烈了。有什么能为您效劳的吗，小姐？”

The young woman looked up at him with eyes dry and mournful. His frank, glowing face, made serious by the gravity of the adventure, his strong, straight figure and the liquid sympathy in his blue eyes, perhaps, also, her imminent need of long-denied help and kindness, thawed her to sudden tears.

"Monsieur," she said, in low tones, "you look to be true and kind. He is my uncle, the brother of my father, and my only relative. He loved my mother, and he hates me because I am like her. He has made my life one long terror. I am afraid of his very looks, and never before dared to disobey him. But tonight he would have married me to a man three times my age. You will forgive me for bringing this vexation upon you, monsieur. You will, of course, decline this mad act he tries to force upon you. But let me thank you for your generous words, at least. I have had none spoken to me in so long."

There was now something more than generosity in the poet's eyes. Poet he must have been, for Yvonne was forgotten; this fine, new loveliness held him with its freshness and grace. The subtle perfume from her filled him with strange emotions. His tender look fell warmly upon her. She leaned to it, thirstily.

"Ten minutes," said David, "is given me in which to do what I would devote years to achieve. I will not say I pity you, mademoiselle; it would not be true—I love you. I cannot ask love from you yet, but let me rescue you from this cruel man, and, in time, love may come. I think I have a future; I will not always be a shepherd. For the present I will cherish you with all my heart and make your life less sad. Will you trust your fate to

年轻女子抬起头，目光呆滞且表情忧郁地看着他。他坦诚而红润的面容，因这场重要的奇遇而变得严肃认真。他体型健壮、身材笔挺，蓝色的双眸里噙着同情的眼泪；而那女子自己长期渴求而不可得的帮助与善意在此刻即将得到满足，这使她突然潸然泪下。

"先生，"她低声说道，"你看上去真诚又善良。他是我叔叔，我父亲的兄弟，也是我唯一的亲人。他爱过我的母亲，因为我长得像她而憎恨我，他让我的生活变得恐怖不堪。我看到他就害怕，从来不敢违背他。但是今晚他要把我嫁给一个比我大两倍的男人。先生，请原谅我把这份烦恼带给你。你当然可以拒绝他这种强人所难的疯狂行为。但是，至少你的慷慨言辞让我为之动容。很久都没人跟我说过这么多的话了。"

在诗人眼里，现在不仅仅是慷慨之情。他肯定是个诗人，因为他早已把伊冯娜忘掉；这位美丽可爱的新交，清新优雅，俘获了他的心。淡雅的香水味使他情愫暗生。他温柔的目光注视着她，充满暖意。而这也是她渴求的。

大卫说："十分钟给了我本需花很多年才能得到的东西。我不想说我可怜你，小姐，那不是我的真心话，我爱你，当然我还不能要求你也爱上我，但是，让我把你从这个残酷的人手中拯救出来吧，也许爱情会随之而来。我相信我的未来一片光明，不会永远做一个牧羊人。现在我要全心全意地珍惜你，让你的人生不再那么悲苦。你愿意把你的人生托付给我吗，小姐？"

me, mademoiselle?"

"Ah, you would sacrifice yourself from pity!"

"From love. The time is almost up, mademoiselle."

"You will regret it, and despise me."

"I will live only to make you happy, and myself worthy of you."

Her fine small hand crept into his from beneath her cloak.

"I will trust you," she breathed, "with my life. And—and love—may not be so far off as you think. Tell him. Once away from the power of his eyes I may forget."

David went and stood before the marquis. The black figure stirred, and the mocking eyes glanced at the great hall clock.

"Two minutes to spare. A shepherd requires eight minutes to decide whether he will accept a bride of beauty and income! Speak up, shepherd, do you consent to become mademoiselle's husband?"

"Mademoiselle," said David, standing proudly, "has done me the honor to yield to my request that she become my wife."

"Well said!" said the marquis. "You have yet the making of a courtier in you, master shepherd. Mademoiselle could have drawn a worse prize, after all. And now to be done with the affair as quick as the Church and the devil will allow!"

He struck the table soundly with his sword hilt. The landlord came, knee-shaking, bringing more candles in the hope of anticipating the great lord's whims. "Fetch a priest," said the marquis, "a priest; do you understand? In ten minutes have a priest here, or—"

“噢，你只是因为同情我而牺牲自己！”

“是因为爱。时间快到了，小姐。”

“你会后悔的，还会憎恨我的。”

“我活着只是为了让你开心，并让自己配得上你。”

她那纤细的手从披风下伸出来，放进他的手里。

“我会信任你，”她轻声说道，“用我的毕生。还有——爱——也许不像你想象的那样遥远。告诉他吧。只要不再看到他凶神恶煞的眼睛，或许我就能忘记过去的一切。”

大卫走到侯爵面前。只见黑色的身影动了动，嘲弄的目光瞥了一眼大厅的钟。

“还剩下两分钟。一个牧羊人竟然需要八分钟来决定他是否接受一位财貌双全的新娘！说吧，牧羊人，你愿意成为这位小姐的丈夫吗？

大卫骄傲地站起来说：“小姐已经屈尊，愿意嫁我为妻，这是我的荣幸。”

“说得好！”侯爵说。“看来你很会奉承嘛，牧羊大师。毕竟小姐可能会遇到更差的人。这事儿得速战速决，只需要教会和魔鬼成全就可以了！”

他用剑柄狠狠地敲着桌子。店主赶来，两膝发抖，拿来更多蜡烛，希望揣摩出大人的怪念头。“找一个神父来，”侯爵说，“一个神父，你明白吗？十分钟后这儿要有个神父，否则——”

The landlord dropped his candles and flew.

The priest came, heavy-eyed and ruffled. He made David Mignot and Lucie de Verennes man and wife, pocketed a gold piece that the marquis tossed him, and shuffled out again into the night.

"Wine," ordered the marquis, spreading his ominous fingers at the host.

"Fill glasses," he said, when it was brought. He stood up at the head of the table in the candlelight, a black mountain of venom and conceit, with something like the memory of an old love turned to poison in his eyes, as it fell upon his niece.

"Monsieur Mignot," he said, raising his wineglass, "drink after I say this to you: You have taken to be your wife one who will make your life a foul and wretched thing. The blood in her is an inheritance running black lies and red ruin. She will bring you shame and anxiety. The devil that descended to her is there in her eyes and skin and mouth that stoop even to beguile a peasant. There is your promise, monsieur poet, for a happy life. Drink your wine. At last, mademoiselle, I am rid of you."

The marquis drank. A little grievous cry, as if from a sudden wound, came from the girl's lips. David, with his glass in his hand, stepped forward three paces and faced the marquis. There was little of a shepherd in his bearing.

"Just now," he said, calmly, "you did me the honor to call me 'monsieur.' May I hope, therefore that my marriage to mademoiselle has placed me somewhat nearer to you in—let us say, reflected rank—has given me the right to stand more as an

店主放下蜡烛便跑了出去。

神父来了，睡眼惺忪，面带愠色。他宣布大卫·米格诺特和露西·德瓦雷斯结为夫妻。随后便将侯爵抛给他的一根金条装进口袋，拖着步子消失在夜色之中。

“上酒。”侯爵命令道，朝店主摊开令人恐惧的手指。

“斟满。”酒刚拿来，他便说道。烛光下，他站在桌子的前面，仿佛一座黑色大山，恶毒又自负。当他望向自己侄女的时候，眼中对于旧爱的追忆瞬间变成了毒药。

“米格诺特先生，”他举起酒杯说道，“听我说完这些，再干了这杯酒：你的妻子会让你的生活变得邪恶污秽，苦不堪言。她的血液里继承了黑色谎言[①]和红色毁灭。她只会使你含羞忍辱，惶惶终日。附在她的眼睛、皮肤和嘴巴里的恶魔充满了邪气，甚至使她愿意屈尊去诱骗一个农夫。诗人先生，这就是你梦寐以求的幸福生活吧。喝酒！最后，小姐，我终于摆脱了你。”

侯爵一饮而尽。女孩发出一声痛苦的叫喊，好像突然受伤了一样。大卫手拿杯子，向前走了三步，面对着侯爵。此时他的神态完全不像一个牧羊人。

“刚才，”他气定神闲地说，“你给我面子，称我‘先生’。因为我和小姐喜结连理，我与你之间的距离稍微近了些——这样说吧，我的这个地位变化——能否让我有权在我脑袋里装着的某件小事上

① 纯粹为了个人利益的谎言称为“黑色谎言”。

equal to monseigneur in a certain little piece of business I have in my mind?"

"You may hope, shepherd," sneered the marquis.

"Then," said David, dashing his glass of wine into the contemptuous[①] eyes that mocked him, "perhaps you will condescend[②] to fight me."

The fury of the great lord outbroke in one sudden curse like a blast from a horn. He tore his sword from its black sheath; he called to the hovering landlord: "A sword there, for this lout!" He turned to the lady, with a laugh that chilled her heart, and said: "You put much labor upon me, Madame. It seems I must find you a husband and make you a widow in the same night."

"I know not sword-play," said David. He flushed to make the confession before his lady.

"'I know not sword-play,'" mimicked the marquis. "Shall we fight like peasants with oaken cudgels? Hola! Francois, my pistols!"

A postilion brought two shining great pistols ornamented with carven silver, from the carriage holsters. The marquis tossed one upon the table near David's hand. "To the other end of the table," he cried; "even a shepherd may pull a trigger. Few of them attain the honor to die by the weapon of a De Beaupertuys."

The shepherd and the marquis faced each other from the ends of the long table. The landlord, in an ague[③] of terror, clutched the air and stammered: "M-M-Monseigneur, for the

① contemptuous *adj.* 轻蔑的，鄙夷的　② condescend *v.* 屈尊，俯就

③ ague *n.* 寒战

与你平起平坐呢？”

“可以，牧羊人。”侯爵冷笑道。

“那么，”大卫说着，把一杯酒泼向那双满含嘲讽之意的双眼，“也许你会屈尊和我决斗。”

侯爵大人一下子火冒三丈，破口大骂，仿佛号角吹响。他把剑从黑鞘里拔出来；冲着在旁边踌躇不安的店主大喊道：“拿剑来，给这个蠢人！”他转向那位小姐，发出令她胆怯的笑声，说道：“你让我为你很是操劳，小姐。看来我一定要在一夜之间，既给你找到丈夫，又让你成为寡妇。”

大卫说：“我不会剑术。”在女士面前坦白，他羞愧得满脸通红。

“我不会剑术。”侯爵嘲弄地模仿他的语调，“难道我们要像农民一样用橡木棍子打架吗？来呀！弗朗索瓦，拿我的手枪来！”

侍从从马车的手枪皮套里拿来两支闪闪发光的镶银手枪。侯爵将其中一支扔到桌上，落在大卫的手边。“到桌子另一边去，”他喊道，“即使是牧羊人也会扣扳机吧。没有几个人有幸死于博贝尔杜依侯爵的枪下。”

牧羊人和侯爵在长桌的两端对立而视。店主惶恐不安，心惊胆战，结结巴巴地说：“大……大……大人，看在上帝的分上，别在我店里干这个呀！——不要流血——那样会毁了我的生意呀——”侯爵凶神恶煞地看着他，顿时使他哑然无声。

love of Christ! not in my house! —do not spill blood—it will ruin my custom—" The look of the marquis, threatening him, paralyzed his tongue.

"Coward," cried the lord of Beaupertuys, "cease chattering your teeth long enough to give the word for us, if you can."

Mine host's knees smote the floor. He was without a vocabulary. Even sounds were beyond him. Still, by gestures he seemed to beseech[1] peace in the name of his house and custom.

"I will give the word," said the lady, in a clear voice. She went up to David and kissed him sweetly. Her eyes were sparkling bright, and color had come to her cheek. She stood against the wall, and the two men leveled their pistols for her count.

"*Un—deux—trois*!"

The two reports came so nearly together that the candles flickered[2] but once. The marquis stood, smiling, the fingers of his left hand resting, outspread, upon the end of the table. David remained erect, and turned his head very slowly, searching for his wife with his eyes. Then, as a garment falls from where it is hung, he sank, crumpled[3], upon the floor.

With a little cry of terror and despair, the widowed maid ran and stooped above him. She found his wound, and then looked up with her old look of pale melancholy. "Through his heart," she whispered. "Oh, his heart!"

"Come," boomed the great voice of the marquis, "out with you to the carriage! Daybreak shall not find you on my hands. Wed you shall be again, and to a living husband, this night. The

---

① beseech v. 恳求，哀求 ② flicker v. 闪烁 ③ crumple v. 崩溃

"懦夫，"博贝尔杜依侯爵大声说道，"牙齿别打战了。有本事，就帮我们发令。"

店主跪到地板上，噤若寒蝉，也听不到任何声音。尽管如此，他仍然双手合十，似乎在为自己的房子和顾客祈求和平和安宁。

"我来发令。"小姐掷地有声地说道。她走到大卫身边，给了他一个甜蜜的亲吻。她星眸璀璨，面若桃花。小姐站在墙边，两个男人举起手枪待命。

"一——二——三！"

两声枪响几乎同时响起，但是烛光只闪烁了一次。侯爵站起来，面带笑容，左手手指叉开放在桌子的后端。大卫保持直立，极其缓慢地转过头，用目光找寻他的妻子。就在这时，如同一件衣服从衣架上掉落下来，他一下子瘫倒在地上。

伴随着一阵恐惧而绝望的哀号，新寡的女士跑过去蹲在他身边。她找到他的伤口，然后抬起那苍白而忧郁的脸。"击中了他的心脏，"她喃喃细语，"哦，他的心脏！"

"出来，"侯爵大声说道，"出来上马车！黎明之前，我非把你嫁出去不可，今晚你会再嫁一次，嫁给活人。小姐，下一次无论我们遇见的是强盗还是农民，你都得嫁给他。如果这条路上别无他人，就

next we come upon, my lady, highwayman or peasant. If the road yields no other, then the churl that opens my gates. Out with you into the carriage!"

The marquis, implacable and huge, the lady wrapped again in the mystery of her cloak, the postilion bearing the weapons—all moved out to the waiting carriage. The sound of its ponderous wheels rolling away echoed through the slumbering village. In the hall of the Silver Flagon the distracted landlord wrung his hands above the slain poet's body, while the flames of the four and twenty candles danced and flickered on the table.

THE RIGHT BRANCH

Three leagues, then, the road ran, and turned into a puzzle. It joined with another and a larger road at right angles. David stood, uncertain, for a while, and then took the road to the right.

Whither it led he knew not, but he was resolved to leave Vernoy far behind that night. He traveled a league and then passed a large chateau which showed testimony of recent entertainment. Lights shone from every window; from the great stone gateway ran a tracery of wheel tracks drawn in the dust by the vehicles of the guests.

Three leagues farther and David was weary. He rested and slept for a while on a bed of pine boughs at the roadside. Then up and on again along the unknown way.

Thus for five days he travelled the great road, sleeping upon Nature's balsamic beds or in peasants' ricks, eating of their black, hospitable bread, drinking from streams or the willing

嫁给我家开门的乡下人。走，上马车！”

大块头的侯爵残酷无情，小姐被迫再一次披上了神秘的披风，马车车队的左马驭手收起武器——所有人出门上了在外等候的马车。笨重车轮滚动的声音在沉睡的村庄里回响。在银壶客栈的大厅里，望着诗人的尸体，心烦意乱的店主不知所措地搓着双手，而桌上二十四根蜡烛的火焰在飘舞闪烁。

右岔路

离这条道三里格的地方是一个岔路口，让人辨不清方向。其中一条更宽的道在这条道的右边。大卫在那儿站了一会儿，不知何去何从，便朝右边走去。

这条路通向哪里他无从知晓，可那晚他已决意要离开维诺伊远走高飞。走了一里格后，他路过一座壮丽的城堡，那里面看起来刚刚结束了一场狂欢。每扇窗户里仍灯火通明。在通向大门的宽敞石路上，载着宾客的马车留下了纵横交错的车轮印。

又走了三里格，大卫感到有些疲倦，便躺在路边的松树枝上休憩片刻。接着，他起身沿着未知的道路继续前行。

就这样，他沿着大道走了五天，途中困了，要么以大地为床，要么就躺到农民的草垛里；饿了，就靠热情好客的农夫给的黑面包充饥；渴了，就从小溪里掬口水喝，或从善良的牧羊人那里得到一杯

cup of the goatherd.

At length he crossed a great bridge and set his foot within the smiling city that has crushed or crowned more poets than all the rest of the world. His breath came quickly as Paris sang to him in a little undertone her vital chant of greeting—the hum of voice and foot and wheel.

High up under the eaves of an old house in the Rue Conti, David paid for lodging, and set himself, in a wooden chair, to his poems. The street, once sheltering citizens of import and consequence, was now given over to those who ever follow in the wake of decline.

The houses were tall and still possessed of a ruined dignity, but many of them were empty save for dust and the spider. By night there was the clash of steel and the cries of brawlers straying restlessly from inn to inn. Where once gentility abode was now but a rancid and rude incontinence. But here David found housing commensurate to his scant purse. Daylight and candlelight found him at pen and paper.

One afternoon he was returning from a foraging trip to the lower world, with bread and curds and a bottle of thin wine. Halfway up his dark stairway he met—or rather came upon, for she rested on the stair—a young woman of a beauty that should balk even the justice of a poet's imagination. A loose, dark cloak, flung open, showed a rich gown beneath. Her eyes changed swiftly with every little shade of thought. Within one moment they would be round and artless like a child's, and long and cozening like a gypsy's. One hand raised her gown,

羊奶。

终于，在跨过了一座大桥后，他走进了这座对他笑脸相迎的城市。这座城市曾为无数的诗人加冕，也令无数诗人的梦想破碎。他仿佛听到了巴黎在为他低声吟唱，不由地心跳加快。人们的说话声、脚步声、车轱辘的声音，交织在一起——欢迎他的到来。

在康帝街的一座老房子里，大卫租了顶楼的一个房间，然后坐到一把木椅上，开始专心写起诗来。这条街上原本住着达官贵人，但如今繁华不在，一片萧条，形形色色的人便来到这里。

这些高高的房子虽破败不堪，却仍保留有几分气派，只是如今大部分的房间都空着没人住，里面已布满灰尘和蜘蛛网。到了晚上，这里响起钢铁的碰撞声，以及爱闹事者出入旅店的高声叫喊声，一片喧嚣。曾经的名流荟萃之所，如今却成为粗野低俗之人聚集的是非之地。但大卫知道自己囊中羞涩，只住得起这种地方。他总是躲在里面俯首写诗，白天写，晚上就着烛光也写。

一天下午，他到楼下买了些面包、炼乳，还有一瓶劣质酒，然后回到破旧的住所。在黑暗的楼梯道里，他走到一半的时候遇到——或者说是邂逅了一位美到不可方物的年轻女郎——她就坐在楼梯上。姿色之美，甚至都超越了诗人的想象。飘逸的黑色披风里面，露出华丽的长裙。她顾盼生辉，眉目传情。本来一双杏眼如孩童般天真无邪，片刻间又变得如吉卜赛人的眼睛那样狡黠细长。她一只手提着长裙，露出一只小小的高跟鞋，原来上面的鞋带松了。她美如天仙，不适合屈尊弯腰；她魅力无穷，分分钟掌控一个男人！也许是她看见大卫来了，就特意待在那里等待帮助吧。

undraping a little shoe, high-heeled, with its ribbons dangling, untied. So heavenly she was, so unfitted to stoop, so qualified to charm and command! Perhaps she had seen David coming, and had waited for his help there.

Ah, would monsieur pardon that she occupied the stairway, but the shoe!—the naughty shoe! Alas! it would not remain tied. Ah! if monsieur would be so gracious!

The poet's fingers trembled as he tied the contrary ribbons. Then he would have fled from the danger of her presence, but the eyes grew long and cozening, like a gypsy's, and held him. He leaned against the balustrade, clutching his bottle of sour wine.

"You have been so good," she said, smiling. "Does monsieur, perhaps, live in the house?"

"Yes, Madame. I—I think so, Madame."

"Perhaps in the third story, then?"

"No, Madame; higher up."

The lady fluttered her fingers with the least possible gesture of impatience.

"Pardon. Certainly I am not discreet in asking. Monsieur will forgive me? It is surely not becoming that I should inquire where he lodges."

"Madame, do not say so. I live in the—"

"No, no, no; do not tell me. Now I see that I erred. But I cannot lose the interest I feel in this house and all that is in it. Once it was my home. Often I come here but to dream of those happy days again. Will you let that be my excuse?"

"Let me tell you, then, for you need no excuse," stammered

唉，请先生别介意她坐在楼梯上，是那只鞋子——那只淘气的鞋子！唉！鞋带松开了！啊！不知道先生可否帮忙！

帮她系鞋带时，诗人的手指微微颤抖。他本该逃之夭夭，但那双似吉卜赛人细长狡黠的眼睛却令他动弹不得。他靠在栏杆上，攥紧他那瓶劣酒。

"你真好。"她笑着说道。"先生，您是否住在这里？"

"是的，女士。我——我是住在这里，女士。"

"是三楼吗？"

"不，女士，我住在更高处。"

这位女士扬了扬手指，没有丝毫的不耐烦。

"抱歉，我并不是有意冒犯才打听的。先生会原谅我吗？我并不是有意打听您的住处。"

"女士，别这么说。我住在——"

"别，别，别，别告诉我。现在我认识到自己错了。不过我还是对这所房子及这里的一切饶有兴趣。这儿曾经是我的家。现在我常回来，只为了回味那旧日美好时光。我这样说您能理解吗？"

"我告诉你吧，你不需要给出任何理由，"诗人结结巴巴地说，

the poet. "I live in the top floor—the small room where the stairs turn."

"In the front room?" asked the lady, turning her head sidewise.

"The rear, Madame."

The lady sighed, as if with relief.

"I will detain you no longer then, monsieur," she said, employing the round and artless eye. "Take good care of my house. Alas! only the memories of it are mine now. Adieu, and accept my thanks for your courtesy."

She was gone, leaving but a smile and a trace of sweet perfume. David climbed the stairs as one in slumber. But he awoke from it, and the smile and the perfume lingered with him and never afterward did either seem quite to leave him. This lady of whom he knew nothing drove him to lyrics of eyes, chansons of swiftly conceived love, odes to curling hair, and sonnets to slippers on slender feet.

Poet he must have been, for Yvonne was forgotten; this fine, new loveliness held him with its freshness and grace. The subtle perfume about her filled him with strange emotions.

On a certain night three persons were gathered about a table in a room on the third floor of the same house. Three chairs and the table and a lighted candle upon it was all the furniture. One of the persons was a huge man, dressed in black. His expression was one of sneering pride. The ends of his upturned moustache reached nearly to his mocking eyes. Another was a lady, young and beautiful, with eyes that could be round and artless, as a

“我住在顶层——楼梯拐角的那个小房间。”

“是前面那间吗？”那位女士问道，把头侧向一边。

“是后面那间，女士。”

女士叹了口气，如释重负的样子。

“那我就不打扰你了，先生。”她转了转她那天真无邪的圆眼睛，说道。“照看好我的房子。唉！现在我对这房子只剩下回忆了。再见，谢谢您的好意。”

她离开了，只留下一个美丽的微笑和一丝甜甜的香水味。大卫如梦游般地爬上楼梯。但清醒过来后，那勾魂的微笑和甜甜的香水味仍一直萦绕在他心头，从此再也不曾忘记。尽管他和这位女士素昧平生，现在却为她诗兴大发。字里行间都在歌咏她那迷人的眼睛，他对她的一见倾心，还有她秀美的卷发。他还用十四行诗吟咏她美丽小脚上的拖鞋。

他肯定是位诗人，因为伊冯娜已从他的脑海中淡去；这位美丽可爱的新交，清新脱俗，彻底让他迷醉。她身上散发出来的那淡雅的香水味使他情愫暗生。

某一天晚上，在这栋房子三楼的同一个房间里，有三个人正围坐在一张桌子旁。三把椅子、一张桌子和桌上那支正在燃烧的蜡烛，便是这房间里的所有物品。三人中有一名大块头的壮汉，身着黑装。他的表情极为倨傲。八字胡两边高高上翘，两端几乎要挨到他那充满嘲弄的眼睛。还有一位女士，年轻貌美，有着一双孩童般圆圆的、天真无邪的大眼睛，但一旦眯缝起来，又似狡黠的吉卜赛人。此刻她也像另外两个密谋的家伙一样，眼神犀利，野心勃勃。

child's, or long and cozening, like a gypsy's, but were now keen and ambitious, like any other conspirator's. The third was a man of action, a combatant, a bold and impatient executive, breathing fire and steel. He was addressed by the others as Captain Desrolles.

This man struck the table with his fist, and said, with controlled violence:

"Tonight. Tonight as he goes to midnight mass. I am tired of the plotting that gets nowhere. I am sick of signals and ciphers and secret meetings and such *baragouin*. Let us be honest traitors. If France is to be rid of him, let us kill in the open, and not hunt with snares and traps. Tonight, I say. I back my words. My hand will do the deed. Tonight, as he goes to mass."

The lady turned upon him a cordial look. Woman, however wedded to plots, must ever thus bow to rash courage. The big man stroked his upturned moustache.

"Dear captain," he said, in a great voice, softened by habit, "this time I agree with you. Nothing is to be gained by waiting. Enough of the palace guards belong to us to make the endeavor a safe one."

"Tonight," repeated Captain Desrolles, again striking the table. "You have heard me, marquis; my hand will do the deed."

"But now," said the huge man, softly, "comes a question. Word must be sent to our partisans in the palace, and a signal agreed upon. Our staunchest men must accompany the royal carriage. At this hour what messenger can penetrate so far as the

第三个是个说干就干的家伙，典型的斗士，大胆而急躁，火气大，性子烈。他被其他人称呼为德斯罗勒斯上尉。

这人用拳头猛击桌子，极力抑制住自己的暴力冲动，说道：

“就定今晚。今晚等他午夜做弥撒时就动手。我早就受够了这漫无目的的策划，厌倦了那些所谓的暗号、密码、秘密会议及毫无意义的讨论。要发动叛乱就无须遮遮掩掩。如果法国要除掉他，那就让我们先开杀吧，别再做什么圈套和陷阱了。就今晚，听着。我说到做到。我会亲自行动。就今晚，等他去做弥撒时就动手。”

那位女士转过身，热忱地看着他。女人啊，一旦参与阴谋，定会被鲁莽之匪气折服。那位壮汉摸了摸他上翘的八字胡。

“亲爱的上尉，”大嗓门的他习惯性压低了声音，“这次我同意你的看法。等来等去是不会有结果的。我们在皇宫里已安插有足够多的人，此次行动必定安全。”

“就今晚吧。”德斯罗勒斯上尉重复道，又一拳捶在桌子上。“你听见了吧，侯爵大人；这次我会亲自动手。”

“可是现在，”大块头男子轻声补充道，“问题来了呢。消息必须送给我们在宫廷的眼线，并统一行动暗号。皇家马车必须由我们的亲信护送。可都到这节骨眼儿上了，哪个信使能一直进到南门口呢？里博特就在那站岗；只要消息传到他那儿，一切都好办了。”

south doorway? Ribouet is stationed there; once a message is placed in his hands, all will go well."

"I will send the message," said the lady.

"You, countess?" said the marquis, raising his eyebrows. "Your devotion is great, we know, but—"

"Listen!" exclaimed the lady, rising and resting her hands upon the table; "in a garret of this house lives a youth from the provinces as guileless and tender as the lambs he tended there. I have met him twice or thrice upon the stairs. I questioned him, fearing that he might dwell too near the room in which we are accustomed to meet. He is mine, if I will. He writes poems in his garret, and I think he dreams of me. He will do what I say. He shall take the message to the palace."

The marquis rose from his chair and bowed. "You did not permit me to finish my sentence, countess," he said. "I would have said: 'Your devotion is great, but your wit and charm are infinitely greater.'"

While the conspirators were thus engaged, David was polishing some lines addressed to his *amorette d'escalier*. He heard a timorous knock at his door, and opened it, with a great throb, to behold her there, panting as one in straits, with eyes wide open and artless, like a child's.

"Monsieur," she breathed, "I come to you in distress. I believe you to be good and true, and I know of no other help. How I flew through the streets among the swaggering men! Monsieur, my mother is dying. My uncle is a captain of guards in the palace of the king. Someone must fly to bring him. May I

“我去送信。”那位女士说。

“你吗，伯爵夫人？”侯爵眉毛上扬，说道。“我们知道，您忠心耿耿，但是——”

“听我说！”女子一下子激动起来，站起来将手放在桌上。“在这栋房子的顶楼，住着不知从哪里来的一位年轻人，跟他照看的羔羊一样天真稚嫩。我在楼道里见过他两三次。曾经担心他的房间离我们常碰头的房间太近，我就问过他住哪里。我可以搞定他，只要我愿意。他成天就待在那阁楼里写诗，而且我看得出他已对我迷恋不已，他会对我言听计从。他能把消息带进宫。”

侯爵从椅子上站起身，鞠了一躬。“请容我把话说完，夫人，”他说道，“我本想说，‘您忠心耿耿，但其实您的智慧与魅力更是无与伦比。’”

在他们密谋造反之时，大卫正在为他写的诗《楼梯爱人》润色。他听见有人轻叩房门，打开一看，心潮澎湃地看到她候在门外，娇喘吁吁，仿佛遇到什么难事。一双大大的眼睛就这么盯着他，像个天真无邪的孩童。

“先生，”她喘着气说，“我遇到困难了。我知道你为人善良，待人真诚，并且现在也没其他人能帮我，所以径直找你来了。大街上到处可见趾高气扬的人，我好不容易穿过街道飞奔过来。先生，我的母亲时日不多。我舅舅是国王的城卫队长，得有人去给他捎个信，我希望——”

hope—"

"Mademoiselle," interrupted David, his eyes shining with the desire to do her service, "your hopes shall be my wings. Tell me how I may reach him."

The lady thrust a sealed paper into his hand.

"Go to the south gate—the south gate, mind—and say to the guards there, 'The falcon has left his nest.' They will pass you, and you will go to the south entrance to the palace. Repeat the words, and give this letter to the man who will reply 'Let him strike when he will.' This is the password, monsieur, entrusted to me by my uncle, for now when the country is disturbed and men plot against the king's life, no one without it can gain entrance to the palace grounds after nightfall. If you will, monsieur, take him this letter so that my mother may see him before she closes her eyes."

"Give it me," said David, eagerly. "But shall I let you return home through the streets alone so late? I—"

"No, no—fly. Each moment is like a precious jewel. Some time," said the lady, with eyes long and cozening, like a gypsy's, "I will try to thank you for your goodness."

The poet thrust the letter into his breast, and bounded down the stairway. The lady, when he was gone, returned to the room below.

The eloquent eyebrows of the marquis interrogated her.

"He is gone," she said, "as fleet and stupid as one of his own sheep, to deliver it."

The table shook again from the batter of Captain

"夫人，"大卫没等她说完，已用眼神告诉她乐意效劳，"您的希望就是我的翅膀。告诉我怎样才能找到他吧。"

那女子把一张密封的信件塞到他的手中。

"去南门——南门——记住——对那里的卫兵说，'鹰已离巢。'他们会放你进去，你可以通过南门进入宫殿。重复刚才那句话，把这封信交给回答"他想出击就让他出击"的人。先生，这是我舅舅留给我的暗号，因为眼下时局动荡，很多人意图谋反杀害国王，你若说不出这个暗号，就不允许在夜幕降临后进入皇宫。先生，如果你愿意的话，请把这封信交给他，这样我的母亲才能在弥留之际见他最后一面。"

"交给我吧，"大卫热切地说，"可都这么晚了，我怎么能让你单独回去呢？我——"

"没事，没事——你赶紧走吧，现在每分每秒都很珍贵。等有机会，"女士说道，一双细长的、狡黠的眼睛，看起来犹如一个吉卜赛人，"我一定好好感谢您的善举。"

诗人把信塞进怀里，冲下楼梯。在他走后，女人回到了楼下的房间。

侯爵抖动着会说话的眉毛，似乎在询问她事情办得怎么样。

"他已出发了，"她说，"犹如他自己喂养的一只羊，傻头傻脑地飞奔而去。"

德斯罗勒斯上尉的拳头捶在了桌子上，桌子又晃动了一下。

Desrolles's fist.

"Sacred name!" he cried; "I have left my pistols behind! I can trust no others."

"Take this," said the marquis, drawing from beneath his cloak a shining, great weapon, ornamented with carven silver. "There are none truer. But guard it closely, for it bears my arms and crest, and already I am suspected. Me, I must put many leagues between myself and Paris this night. Tomorrow must find me in my chateau. After you, dear countess."

The marquis puffed out the candle. The lady, well cloaked, and the two gentlemen softly descended the stairway and flowed into the crowd that roamed along the narrow pavements of the Rue Conti.

David sped. At the south gate of the king's residence a halberd was laid to his breast, but he turned its point with the words; "The falcon has left his nest."

"Pass, brother," said the guard, "and go quickly."

On the south steps of the palace they moved to seize him, but again the *mot de passé* charmed the watchers. One among them stepped forward and began: "Let him strike—" but a flurry among the guards told of a surprise. A man of keen look and soldierly stride suddenly pressed through them and seized the letter which David held in his hand. "Come with me," he said, and led him inside the great hall. Then he tore open the letter and read it. He beckoned to a man uniformed as an officer of musketeers, who was passing. "Captain Tetreau, you will have the guards at the south entrance and the south gate arrested

“上帝啊！”他大声说道。“我忘记带手枪了！谁动手我都觉得不可靠。”

“拿着。”侯爵边说边从他的披风下面拿出一支闪闪发光的镶银手枪。“没有什么比这个更实在了，但你要好好保管它，这上面有我的纹章和徽号，我已经被怀疑了。今晚我得远离巴黎，明天要回到我的城堡。你先走吧，亲爱的伯爵夫人。”

侯爵一口气吹灭了蜡烛。这位女士将自己裹得严严实实，和两位先生轻手轻脚地走下楼梯，汇入康帝街狭窄的街道上拥挤的人潮中。

大卫一路飞奔。刚到皇宫的南门，一根长戟就抵在他的胸前，他快速说出了口令，“鹰已离巢。”

“进去吧，兄弟，”卫兵说，“快走。”

在宫殿南边的台阶上，又有卫兵们截住了他，那口令再次奏效。其中一个卫兵站出来说：“他想出击——”但是卫兵中间突然一阵骚动，说明他们感到不妙。一个眼神犀利的战士突然向前跨步，站到其他人的前面，夺过大卫手里拿着的那封信。“跟我来。”他说道，将大卫带到一个大厅。然后，他拆开信件看了一遍，看见一名火枪手军官模样的人由此经过，便朝他挥挥手。“泰特罗上尉，你去南大门，把那儿的卫兵们都逮捕关押起来，换成我们的亲信。”然后他对大卫说：“跟我走。”

and confined. Place men known to be loyal in their places." To David he said: "Come with me."

He conducted him through a corridor and an anteroom into a spacious chamber, where a melancholy man, sombrely dressed, sat brooding in a great, leather-covered chair. To that man he said:

"Sire, I have told you that the palace is as full of traitors and spies as a sewer is of rats. You have thought, sire, that it was my fancy. This man penetrated to your very door by their connivance. He bore a letter which I have intercepted. I have brought him here that your majesty may no longer think my zeal excessive."

"I will question him," said the king, stirring in his chair. He looked at David with heavy eyes dulled by an opaque film. The poet bent his knee.

"From where do you come?" asked the king.

"From the village of Vernoy, in the province of Eure-et-Loir, sire."

"What do you follow in Paris?"

"I—I would be a poet, sire."

"What did you in Vernoy?"

"I minded my father's flock of sheep."

The king stirred again, and the film lifted from his eyes.

"Ah! in the fields!"

"Yes, sire."

"You lived in the fields; you went out in the cool of the morning and lay among the hedges in the grass. The flock

他领着大卫穿过走廊和前厅，来到一间宽敞的大厅里，一位穿着深色衣服、面色忧郁的男子坐在一张豪华真皮座椅上沉思。只听领路人对那人说：

“陛下，臣曾进言说宫内的叛徒和间谍，犹如下水管道的老鼠一样多。陛下却以为臣言过其实，此人就是得益于他们的帮助，竟一路畅通无阻地来到您的宫殿门前。臣已截获了他带的那封信，并把此人带来。臣是否言过其实，还请陛下明鉴。”

“我来审问一下他。”国王说着，在椅子上挪了挪身子。他看着大卫，眼神疲惫，目光迷离。诗人屈膝下跪。

“你从哪里来？”国王问。

“厄尔卢瓦尔省维诺伊村，陛下。”

“来巴黎做什么？”

“我——我想成为一位诗人，陛下。”

“家中以何营生？”

“帮我父亲放羊。”

国王再次挪动身子，眼里突现神采。

“噢！在田野间！”

“是的，陛下。”

“你既生活在这田野间，待拂晓外出，凉风习习，可躺卧在青草之上，任羊群散布，星星点点；你可饮那甘甜溪水，坐于树下品尝美

distributed itself upon the hillside; you drank of the living stream; you ate your sweet, brown bread in the shade, and you listened, doubtless, to blackbirds piping in the grove. Is not that so, shepherd?"

"It is, sire," answered David, with a sigh; "and to the bees at the flowers, and, maybe, to the grape gatherers singing on the hill."

"Yes, yes," said the king, impatiently; "maybe to them; but surely to the blackbirds. They whistled often, in the grove, did they not?"

"Nowhere, sire, so sweetly as in Eure-et-Loir. I have endeavored to express their song in some verses that I have written."

"Can you repeat those verses?" asked the king, eagerly. "A long time ago I listened to the blackbirds. It would be something better than a kingdom if one could rightly construe their song. And at night you drove the sheep to the fold and then sat, in peace and tranquility, to your pleasant bread. Can you repeat those verses, shepherd?"

"They run this way, sire," said David, with respectful ardor:

Lazy shepherd, see your lambkins
Skip, ecstatic, on the mead;
See the firs dance in the breezes,
Hear Pan blowing at his reed.

Hear us calling from the tree-tops,

味面包，还可画眉鸟婉转于树林。对吗，牧羊人？”

“是的，陛下，”大卫叹了口气，回答道，“还听见蜜蜂在花丛中嗡嗡嗡地唱歌，有时还能听见山上传来葡萄采摘者的动听歌声。”

“知道了，知道了，”国王不耐烦地说道，“或许可以听见他们，不过，毋庸置疑，定会是有画眉。画眉婉转于林间，是不是？”

“尤里爱特卢瓦的画眉唱得最甜美动听，我曾写诗来重现它们的歌声。”

“可否为我吟诵几句？”国王热切地问道。“犹记当年，我也曾闻画眉啼鸣。若有人能将其歌声细细描绘，可比坐拥一个国还强。入夜，你驱羊入圈，坐下即可品尝香甜的面包，宁静而安详。牧羊人，可愿为我吟诵几句？”

“诗是这样写的，陛下，”大卫恭敬而又激动地吟诵道，

懒惰的牧羊人，看看你的羊宝宝们
欢呼雀跃在这草地
看那枞树随微风起舞
听潘恩吹响他的芦笛

听我们来自树梢的呼喊

See us swoop upon your flock;

Yield us wool to make our nests warm in the branches of the—

"If it please your majesty," interrupted a harsh voice, "I will ask a question or two of this rhymester. There is little time to spare. I crave pardon, sire, if my anxiety for your safety offends."

"The loyalty," said the king, "of the Duke d'Aumale is too well proven to give offence." He sank into his chair, and the film came again over his eyes.

"First," said the duke, "I will read you the letter he brought:

'Tonight is the anniversary of the dauphin's death. If he goes, as is his custom, to midnight mass to pray for the soul of his son, the falcon will strike, at the corner of the Rue Esplanade. If this be his intention, set a red light in the upper room at the southwest corner of the palace, that the falcon may take heed.'"

"Peasant," said the duke, sternly, "you have heard these words. Who gave you this message to bring?"

"My lord duke," said David, sincerely, "I will tell you. A lady gave it me. She said her mother was ill, and that this writing would fetch her uncle to her bedside. I do not know the meaning of the letter, but I will swear that she is beautiful and good."

"Describe the woman," commanded the duke, "and how you came to be her dupe."

看我们掠过你的羊群

给我们一些羊毛筑巢取暖

在这树杈之间——

“回禀陛下，”一个沙哑的声音打断了他的朗诵，“容我问这蹩脚诗人一两个问题。时间紧迫，臣自知多有冒犯，还请陛下宽恕。”

国王道：“多马尔公爵自当对我忠心耿耿，谈不上冒犯。”他整个身子陷进了椅子里，目光中又闪现出久违的神采。

“首先，”公爵说，“容我为您朗读他带来的这封信：

‘今晚是皇太子的忌日，若他照往常一样去做午夜弥撒，去为他儿子的灵魂祷告，那么猎鹰将在滨海广场的拐角处发起攻击。如果他确有此打算，就在宫殿西南角楼上房间里点上一盏红灯，这样猎鹰就能看到。’”

“乡下人，”公爵厉声说道，“你也听到这些话了。是谁让送信进来的？”

“公爵大人，”大卫一脸真诚地说，“我可以都告诉您。是一位女士托付我的。她说她的母亲病危，所以需要把这封信交给他舅舅。我虽不知信的内容，但我保证，她既美丽又善良。”

“描述一下那个女人，”公爵命令道，“还有你是怎么上了她的圈套的。”

"Describe her!" said David with a tender smile. "You would command words to perform miracles. Well, she is made of sunshine and deep shade. She is slender, like the alders, and moves with their grace. Her eyes change while you gaze into them; now round, and then half shut as the sun peeps between two clouds. When she comes, heaven is all about her; when she leaves, there is chaos and a scent of hawthorn blossoms. She came to see me in the Rue Conti, number twenty-nine."

"It is the house," said the duke, turning to the king, "that we have been watching. Thanks to the poet's tongue, we have a picture of the infamous Countess Quebedaux."

"Sire and my lord duke," said David, earnestly, "I hope my poor words have done no injustice. I have looked into that lady's eyes. I will stake my life that she is an angel, letter or no letter."

The duke looked at him steadily. "I will put you to the proof," he said, slowly. "Dressed as the king, you shall, yourself, attend mass in his carriage at midnight. Do you accept the test?"

David smiled. "I have looked into her eyes," he said. "I had my proof there. Take yours how you will."

Half an hour before twelve the Duke d'Aumale, with his own hands, set a red lamp in a southwest window of the palace. At ten minutes to the hour, David, leaning on his arm, dressed as the king, from top to toe, with his head bowed in his cloak, walked slowly from the royal apartments to the waiting carriage. The duke assisted him inside and closed the door. The carriage whirled away along its route to the cathedral.

On the *qui vive* in a house at the corner of the Rue

"描述一下她！"大卫温柔地笑着说。"你这是在命令语言来创造奇迹。好吧，她有时如明媚的阳光，有时若阴郁的色彩。她身材苗条，亭亭玉立。行走时如扶风杨柳，婀娜多姿。她明眸轻眨，如微云遮月，使人不由驻足凝视。她来时，似九天玄女；离开时，仍弥留幽兰醇香。她来我的住处找到我，在康帝街二十九号。"

"就是那栋房子，"公爵转身对国王说，"我们一直在监视。亏得他能说会道，我们把那个伤风败俗的奎北道斯伯爵夫人的情况弄得清清楚楚。"

"尊敬的陛下，公爵，"大卫神情恳切地说，"小人笨嘴拙舌，希望没有影响到大人的正确判断。可是，那位小姐的眼神清澈无比，就像圣洁的天使，我愿为她赌上性命，和捎不捎信没有关系。"

公爵一眼不眨地看着他。"我会让你看到她的真面目，"他慢慢说道，"今夜，你就打扮成国王的模样，坐着国王的马车去做弥撒。愿意接受这个试验吗？"

大卫笑了。他说："我能看透她的眼睛，我自己心中有数。你自己也去弄清楚吧。"

十一时半，多马尔公爵亲手在宫殿西南方的窗台上放了一盏红灯。二十分钟后，大卫从头到脚都打扮成国王的样子，披着披风，由多马尔公爵扶着，低着头走出皇家宫殿，缓慢走向等候在外的马车。公爵扶他上车，并关好马车门。马车朝着大教堂的方向飞奔而去。

在滨海广场拐角处的房子里，泰特罗上尉和另外二十人在此蹲

Esplanade was Captain Tetreau with twenty men, ready to pounce upon the conspirators when they should appear.

But it seemed that, for some reason, the plotters had slightly altered their plans. When the royal carriage had reached the Rue Christopher, one square nearer than the Rue Esplanade, forth from it burst Captain Desrolles, with his band of would-be regicides, and assailed the equipage. The guards upon the carriage, though surprised at the premature attack, descended and fought valiantly. The noise of conflict attracted the force of Captain Tetreau, and they came pelting down the street to the rescue. But, in the meantime, the desperate Desrolles had torn open the door of the king's carriage, thrust his weapon against the body of the dark figure inside, and fired.

Now, with loyal reinforcements at hand, the street rang with cries and the rasp of steel, but the frightened horses had dashed away. Upon the cushions lay the dead body of the poor mock king and poet, slain by a ball from the pistol of Monseigneur, the Marquis de Beaupertuys.

THE MAIN ROAD

Three leagues, then, the road ran, and turned into a puzzle. It joined with another and a larger road at right angles. David stood, uncertain, for a while, and then sat himself to rest upon its side.

Whither these roads led he knew not. Either way there seemed to lie a great world full of chance and peril. And then, sitting there, his eye fell upon a bright star, one that he and

守，准备在谋反分子出现时将他们捕获。

可是，不知某种原因，谋反者们似乎改变了他们的计划。当皇家马车到达克里斯托弗大街，比滨海广场更近的一个街心广场时，遭到了德斯罗斯上尉和他手下的一群弑君同谋者的偷袭。马车上的警卫，虽然对这提早的袭击感到惊讶，却依旧勇敢地下车应战。双方冲突的喧嚣引来了泰特罗上尉的部队，他们沿街赶来救援。与此同时，誓决一死的德斯罗勒斯上尉撞开马车门，端起武器朝里面的黑影射击。

随着忠于国王的护卫部队的不断增援，大街上的喊杀声、刀剑的撞击声，连成一片，但受惊的御马早已狂奔而去。马车坐垫上躺着假扮国王的倒霉诗人的尸体，是被博贝尔杜依侯爵的手枪射出的一发子弹击中毙命的。

主干道

离这条道三里格的地方是一个岔路口，让人迷糊辨不清方向。其中一条更宽的道与这条道垂直相交。大卫在那儿站了一会儿，不知何去何从，便坐在路边休息。

这些道路通往何处，大卫无从知晓。但无论选择哪一条，似乎机遇与危险同在。大卫坐在那儿，抬头仰望天空中一颗明亮的星星，那是他和伊冯娜一起命名的。他不禁想起伊冯娜，不知道他的

Yvonne had named for theirs. That set him thinking of Yvonne, and he wondered if he had not been too hasty. Why should he leave her and his home because a few hot words had come between them? Was love so brittle a thing that jealousy, the very proof of it, could break it? Mornings always brought a cure for the little heartaches of evening. There was yet time for him to return home without any one in the sweetly sleeping village of Vernoy being the wiser. His heart was Yvonne's; there where he had lived always he could write his poems and find his happiness.

David rose, and shook off his unrest and the wild mood that had tempted him. He set his face steadfastly back along the road he had come. By the time he had retraveled the road to Vernoy, his desire to rove was gone. He passed the sheepfold, and the sheep scurried, with a drumming flutter, at his late footsteps, warming his heart by the homely sound. He crept without noise into his little room and lay there, thankful that his feet had escaped the distress of new roads that night.

How well he knew woman's heart! The next evening Yvonne was at the well in the road where the young congregated in order that the *cure* might have business. The corner of her eye was engaged in a search for David, albeit her set mouth seemed unrelenting. He saw the look; braved the mouth, drew from it a recantation and, later, a kiss as they walked homeward together.

Three months afterwards they were married. David's father was shrewd and prosperous. He gave them a wedding that was heard of three leagues away. Both the young people were

所作所为是否过于草率。难道仅仅因为几句拌嘴，便要与她分手，甚至离家出走？难道爱情如此脆弱，仅因嫉妒——这本来是爱情存在的证据，就能让爱破碎？前一晚有过的小小心痛，过一夜总会自动痊愈。他现在回家还不晚，毕竟沉睡在甜美梦乡的村民还不知他此刻已离家出走了呢。伊冯娜是他心之所属，在他自幼生活着的村子里，他可以写诗，可以找到自己的幸福。

大卫站起身，摆脱了之前引诱他的不安情绪和胡思乱想。他转身坚定地向着来时的路往回走。当他回到维诺伊村时，想浪迹天涯的想法已全然消失。他穿过羊圈，羊群听到了他半夜的脚步声，急匆匆地跑过来，发出类似鼓点的脚步声，这熟悉的声音温暖了他的心。他蹑手蹑脚地溜进自己的房间躺下，庆幸自己的双脚免遭新征途的劳役之苦。

他太了解女人的心思了！第二天晚上，伊冯娜站在路边的水井旁，那里是年轻人聚在一起听牧师讲道的地方。尽管还倔强地噘着嘴，其实她一直在用眼角的余光寻找大卫。见此场景，他鼓起勇气上前，结果不仅获得了谅解，一起回家的路上，还得到了一个香吻。

三个月后他们结婚了。大卫的父亲不仅精明能干，还很富有。他为他们举办了一场豪华婚礼，那场面之大连三里格之外的人都听说了。村里人都喜欢这对新人。他们在大街上排队贺喜，在绿茵草

favorites in the village. There was a procession in the streets, a dance on the green; they had the marionettes and a tumbler out from Dreux to delight the guests.

Then a year, and David's father died. The sheep and the cottage descended to him. He already had the seemliest wife in the village. Yvonne's milk pails and her brass kettles were bright—*ouf*! they blinded you in the sun when you passed that way. But you must keep your eyes upon her yard, for her flower beds were so neat and gay they restored to you your sight. And you might hear her sing, aye, as far as the double chestnut tree above Père Gruneau's blacksmith forge.

But a day came when David drew out paper from a long-shut drawer, and began to bite the end of a pencil. Spring had come again and touched his heart. Poet he must have been, for now Yvonne was well-nigh forgotten. This fine new loveliness of earth held him with its witchery and grace. The perfume from her woods and meadows stirred him strangely. Daily had he gone forth with his flock, and brought it safe at night. But now he stretched himself under the hedge and pieced words together on his bits of paper. The sheep strayed, and the wolves, perceiving that difficult poems make easy mutton, ventured from the woods and stole his lambs.

David's stock of poems grew longer and his flock smaller. Yvonne's nose and temper waxed sharp and her talk blunt. Her pans and kettles grew dull, but her eyes had caught their flash. She pointed out to the poet that his neglect was reducing the flock and bringing woe upon the household. David hired a boy to

地上欢舞；还从德卢克斯请来了牵线木偶和杂技演员给客人们助兴。

一年后，大卫的父亲去世了。羊群和农舍都传给了他。他已经拥有村里最漂亮贤淑的妻子。伊冯娜总是把奶桶和铜水壶擦得锃亮！在阳光下，当你走过她家的那条道时，它们的光亮会刺得你睁不开眼。但是你还要记得看看她家的院子，花坛修剪得十分整齐，鲜花五颜六色地开放，不由地令你眼前一亮。你可能还会有幸听到她放声歌唱，在佩雷·格鲁诺铁匠铺顶上的两棵并排生长的板栗树上都能听得一清二楚。

可是有一天，大卫打开一个许久未开的抽屉，从里面抽出一张纸来，又开始咬住那铅笔头，埋头写起诗来。春天又来了，他的心也苏醒了。他肯定是位诗人，而伊冯娜被完全抛在脑后。大地万象更新，处处是新颜，不由得让他着魔。树丛和草地上的香气弥漫，使他心生波澜。以前他白天放羊，晚上再将羊群安全带回。可现在，他栖身树篱下，在纸片上拼凑文字。羊群四处游走，给了狼可乘之机，从树林里冒出来，掳走他的羔羊。

大卫写的诗越来越多，但羊群却愈放愈少。伊冯娜的脾气变得暴躁，说话也日渐生硬。她的锅和水壶生了锈，可是眼神却愈趋犀利。她向诗人指出是他的疏忽导致羊越来越少，给家庭带来不幸。于是大卫请了一个男孩来守护羊群，把自己锁在阁楼里，写出了更多的诗。那个男孩天生是个诗人，奈何没有合适的契机，就整日昏

guard the sheep, locked himself in the little room at the top of the cottage, and wrote more poems. The boy, being a poet by nature, but not furnished with an outlet in the way of writing, spent his time in slumber. The wolves lost no time in discovering that poetry and sleep are practically the same; so the flock steadily grew smaller. Yvonne's ill temper increased at an equal rate. Sometimes she would stand in the yard and rail at David through his high window. Then you could hear her as far as the double chestnut tree above Pere Gruneau's blacksmith forge.

M. Papineau, the kind, wise, meddling old notary, saw this, as he saw everything at which his nose pointed. He went to David, fortified himself with a great pinch of snuff, and said:

"Friend Mignot, I affixed the seal upon the marriage certificate of your father. It would distress me to be obliged to attest a paper signifying the bankruptcy of his son. But that is what you are coming to. I speak as an old friend. Now, listen to what I have to say. You have your heart set, I perceive, upon poetry. At Dreux, I have a friend, one Monsieur Bril—Georges Bril. He lives in a little cleared space in a houseful of books. He is a learned man; he visits Paris each year; he himself has written books. He will tell you when the catacombs were made, how they found out the names of the stars, and why the plover has a long bill. The meaning and the form of poetry is to him as intelligent as the baa of a sheep is to you. I will give you a letter to him, and you shall take him your poems and let him read them. Then you will know if you shall write more, or give your attention to your wife and business."

昏然地度过。狼群发现爱写诗的人无异于贪睡觉的人，所以继续伺机掠走一只又一只羊。伊冯娜的脾气也随之越变越坏。有时她会站在院子里，透过阁楼的窗子大声呵斥大卫。人们在佩雷·格鲁诺铁匠铺顶上那两棵并排长着的板栗树上都能听到那骂声。

帕皮诺老先生，这位聪明善良、爱管闲事的公证人，敏锐地注意到了这一点，一切都逃不过他的眼睛。他跑去大卫家，深吸了一大口气后说道：

“米格诺特，我亲爱的朋友，你父亲结婚证上的公章还是我盖的。若我要迫不得已为他儿子作破产公证，那会让我很难过的。但这正是你即将面临的困境。我以老朋友的身份说几句，你要认真听。我知道，你一门心思想做个诗人。在德勒，我有一个朋友，布里尔先生——乔治·布里尔。他的家里堆满了书籍，只剩下一小块落脚之地。他学识渊博，每年都要去巴黎，他自己也写书。他能告诉你地下墓穴是什么时候建造的，人们是如何发现星星的名字的，以及为什么啄木鸟有着长长的嘴巴。他对诗的意义和形式的了解程度，比得上你对羊的咩咩声的熟悉程度，我写封信给你带去，你把你的诗也带上让他读读。随后你就能知道是应该继续写诗，还是把注意力放在你的妻子和事业上。”

"Write the letter," said David, "I am sorry you did not speak of this sooner."

At sunrise the next morning he was on the road to Dreux with the precious roll of poems under his arm. At noon he wiped the dust from his feet at the door of Monsieur Bril. That learned man broke the seal of M. Papineau's letter, and sucked up its contents through his gleaming spectacles as the sun draws water. He took David inside to his study and sat him down upon a little island beat upon by a sea of books.

Monsieur Bril had a conscience. He flinched not even at a mass of manuscript the thickness of a finger-length and rolled to an incorrigible curve. He broke the back of the roll against his knee and began to read. He slighted nothing; he bored into the lump as a worm into a nut, seeking for a kernel.

Meanwhile, David sat, marooned, trembling in the spray of so much literature. It roared in his ears. He held no chart or compass for voyaging in that sea. Half the world, he thought, must be writing books.

Monsieur Bril bored to the last page of the poems. Then he took off his spectacles, and wiped them with his handkerchief.

"My old friend, Papineau, is well?" he asked.

"In the best of health," said David.

"How many sheep have you, Monsieur Mignot?"

"Three hundred and nine, when I counted them yesterday. The flock has had ill fortune. To that number it has decreased from eight hundred and fifty."

"You have a wife and home, and lived in comfort. The

“那你快写信吧，”大卫说，“为何不早说呢？”

第二天太阳刚出来，他便夹着珍爱的诗卷踏上了去德勒的路。中午，他在布里尔先生的家门口擦净脚上的灰尘。那位学识渊博之人开启帕皮诺先生的信，犹如太阳吸干水分一般，透过闪闪发光的眼镜吸透了信的内容。他把大卫带到书房里，从书海里腾出一小块儿空地，让他坐下。

布里尔先生十分尽心尽力。面对一指厚卷作一团的手稿，他都不厌其烦。他把诗卷摊开，放在膝盖上，开始阅读。他十分认真地读完每一首诗，那全神贯注的样子就像一只虫子钻进坚果里寻找果仁一样。

与此同时，大卫坐在那里，感觉置身于一座孤岛，面对四周的茫茫书海，不禁心生焦虑。浩瀚的文字翻卷起朵朵浪花，在他耳边咆哮。而在这书海里航行，他既无地图也无指南针。他心想，世界上肯定有一半的人都在写书吧。

布里尔先生读完了诗卷的最后一页。这时，他摘下眼镜，用手帕擦了擦。

“我的老朋友帕皮诺，他还好吗？”他问。

“非常好。”大卫说。

“你有多少只羊，米格诺特先生？”

“三百零九只，昨天刚数过。不幸得很，原来有八百五十只，现在只剩这么多了。”

“你已成家立业，过着幸福美满的生活。羊群带给你很多。你

sheep brought you plenty. You went into the fields with them and lived in the keen air and ate the sweet bread of contentment. You had but to be vigilant and recline there upon nature's breast, listening to the whistle of the blackbirds in the grove. Am I right thus far?"

"It was so," said David.

"I have read all your verses," continued Monsieur Bril, his eyes wandering about his sea of books as if he conned the horizon for a sail. "Look yonder, through that window, Monsieur Mignot; tell me what you see in that tree."

"I see a crow," said David, looking.

"There is a bird," said Monsieur Bril, "that shall assist me where I am disposed to shirk a duty. You know that bird, Monsieur Mignot; he is the philosopher of the air. He is happy through submission to his lot. None so merry or full-crawed as he with his whimsical eye and rollicking step. The fields yield him what he desires. He never grieves that his plumage is not gay, like the oriole's. And you have heard, Monsieur Mignot, the notes that nature has given him? Is the nightingale any happier, do you think?"

David rose to his feet. The crow cawed harshly from his tree.

"I thank you, Monsieur Bril," he said, slowly. "There was not, then, one nightingale among all those croaks?"

"I could not have missed it," said Monsieur Bril, with a sigh. "I read every word. Live your poetry, man; do not try to write it any more."

与它们一起走进田野，呼吸清新的空气，品尝美味的面包。你只需要提高警惕，躺在大自然的怀抱中，听着树林里画眉的鸣声。我说的这些对吗？”

“的确如此。”大卫说。

“我已经读完了你所有的诗歌。”布里尔先生继续说，目光徘徊在他的书海之中，就如同眺望天边的一艘帆船。“看看窗外远处的地方，米格诺特先生，告诉我你在那棵树上看见了什么？”

“我看见了一只乌鸦。”大卫目视远方说。

“就是那只鸟，”布里尔先生说，“在我想推卸责任的时候它可以帮到我。你知道那只鸟吧，米格诺特先生；它是空中的哲学家。它乐于天命。没有谁像它那么高兴，也没有谁像它那么满足，它总是有着古怪精灵般的目光和欢乐无忧的步伐。它想要什么，大地就给它什么。它从不因自己的羽毛不如黄鹂的绚丽多彩而悲伤。而且你听过大自然赋予它的声音，米格诺特先生，你认为夜莺比它更快乐吗？”

大卫站了起来。乌鸦在树上发出刺耳的呱呱声。

“谢谢你，布里尔先生。”他慢慢说道。“那么，在这些呱呱的叫声中，难道就从来没有夜莺的歌声吗？”

“如果有，我一定会听见。”布里尔先生叹了口气说。“我品读了你写的每一个字。小伙子，诗意地生活吧，但不要再写诗了。”

"I thank you," said David, again. "And now I will be going back to my sheep."

"If you would dine with me," said the man of books, "and overlook the smart of it, I will give you reasons at length."

"No," said the poet, "I must be back in the fields cawing at my sheep."

Back along the road to Vernoy he trudged with his poems under his arm. When he reached his village he turned into the shop of one Zeigler, a Jew out of Armenia, who sold anything that came to his hand.

"Friend," said David, "wolves from the forest harass my sheep on the hills. I must purchase firearms to protect them. What have you?"

"A bad day, this, for me, friend Mignot," said Zeigler, spreading his hands, "for I perceive that I must sell you a weapon that will not fetch a tenth of its value. Only last week I bought from a peddler a wagon full of goods that he procured at a sale by a *commissionaire* of the crown. The sale was of the *chateau* and belongings of a great lord—I know not his title—who has been banished for conspiracy against the king. There are some choice firearms in the lot. This pistol—oh, a weapon fit for a prince!—it shall be only forty francs to you, friend Mignot—if I lose ten by the sale. But perhaps an arquebuse—"

"This will do," said David, throwing the money on the counter. "Is it charged?"

"I will charge it," said Zeigler. "And, for ten francs more, add a store of powder and ball."

“谢谢你。”大卫又说。“现在我得回去放羊了。”

“如果你愿意和我一起吃饭，”这位有学识之人说道，“又不怕忠言逆耳，我可以为你细细道来。”

“不了，”诗人说，“我必须回到田野去，像乌鸦呱呱叫一样，我也要守着我的羊群。”

在回维诺伊的路上，他把诗卷夹在手臂下，步履沉重。回到村子后，他拐进了齐格勒家开的商店。齐格勒是来自亚美尼亚的犹太人。凡是到手的东西都卖。

“朋友，”大卫说，“森林中的狼跑到山上来骚扰我的羊群。我得买支枪来保护它们。你有什么枪？”

“今天生意不景气，我的朋友米格诺特，”齐格勒摊开双手说，“这里有把枪，我以不足原价十分之一的价格卖给你吧，上周我刚从一个小贩那里买来一车货，是一个皇室看门人低价卖给他的。据说那位看门人出售的是一位侯爵的城堡和财产——我不知道他的头衔——他因为谋反罪遭国王流放。这里有一些上好的枪支，这把手枪——哦，简直配得上王子的身份——我只收你四十法郎——米格诺特朋友，我给你倒赔十块呢，这还有把火绳枪——”

“就它吧，”大卫说，把钱扔在柜台上，“装子弹了吗？”

“我这就装，”齐格勒说，“火药和子弹，另需十法郎。”

David laid his pistol under his coat and walked to his cottage. Yvonne was not there. Of late she had taken to gadding much among the neighbors. But a fire was glowing in the kitchen stove. David opened the door of it and thrust his poems in upon the coals. As they blazed up they made a singing, harsh sound in the flue.

"The song of the crow!" said the poet.

He went up to his attic room and closed the door. So quiet was the village that a score of people heard the roar of the great pistol. They flocked thither, and up the stairs where the smoke, issuing, drew their notice.

The men laid the body of the poet upon his bed, awkwardly arranging it to conceal the torn plumage of the poor black crow. The women chattered in a luxury of zealous pity. Some of them ran to tell Yvonne.

M. Papineau, whose nose had brought him there among the first, picked up the weapon and ran his eye over its silver mountings with a mingled air of connoisseurship and grief.

"The arms," he explained, aside, to the *cure*, "and crest of Monseigneur, the Marquis de Beaupertuys."

大卫把手枪放在外套下面，回到他的小屋。伊冯娜不在家。最近她经常去邻居家串门。但炉灶里的火还燃着。大卫打开灶门，把他的诗卷扔进炉火中。它们迅速燃烧，发出一种如歌的嘶嘶声。

"乌鸦之歌！"诗人说。

他走到阁楼上的房间，关上门。村子里很安静，好多人听到了枪"砰"的一声巨响。他们循声来到了大卫家，一起涌上楼梯，正是楼上冒着的烟吸引了他们的注意。

男人们将诗人的尸体抱上床，笨拙地收拾好，没让这只可怜的黑乌鸦露出被撕裂的羽毛。女人们则窃窃私语，流露出无限同情，有几个人跑去通知伊冯娜。

嗅觉灵敏的帕皮诺先生也在第一时间赶到了这里。他拿起那把枪，眼睛盯着银雕装饰，一边对其品质进行鉴赏，一边表露出悲哀的情绪。

"这把手枪，"他对一旁的神父解释道，"上面有博贝尔杜依侯爵的徽号。"

The Furnished Room
带家具的出租屋

在纽约下西区的一片破烂不堪的红砖大楼中，一名年轻男子在此往来穿梭。没有人知道他从何而来，只知道他要在这座“如巨大流沙堆的城市”寻找他那“离家出走”的挚爱。他在此历经数月，跑遍了这里的每一家剧院和音乐厅，却依然一无所获。为了便于找寻，他在第十二栋楼的女房东那里租了一间带家具的出租屋。在那间出租屋里，年轻人意外感受到了爱人的气息，听到了爱人的“呼唤”。他找遍房子的每一个角落，希望能够找到爱人在此住过的些许痕迹，但终究一无所获。当他满怀希望地询问房东时，却得到了一成不变的否定回复。“希望如潮水退去，信念也渐渐枯竭”，绝望的男子回到房间自杀身故。而在故事的结尾，我们在房东的闲聊中得知，男子苦苦寻觅的爱人于一周前在同一间出租屋里以同样的方式结束了自己的生命。出乎意料的故事结局延续了欧·亨利一贯的叙事风格。在一个物欲横流的年代，人们都成了为生活所累的匆匆过客。人际温情被异化，爱与深情变得一文不名。年轻人为爱而来，最终却陈尸出租屋。年轻人因何而死？是对挚爱一往情深而不得的绝望，还是女房东只为金钱而不近人情的欺骗？男子的挚爱又是因何而死？是为了自己的演员梦，还是因为现实生活的残酷？我们不得尽知。唯一知晓的是在一个金钱遍地的都市，两条鲜活生命的消殒诉说了一个悲情残酷的故事。故事凄凉悲冷，只有男子心中对爱人那一往情深的牵念是故事唯一的温情。而故事背后言说的人情冷暖、金钱利益、家园追寻以及生活艰辛，唯有留待读者去细读细品。

Restless, shifting, fugacious as time itself is a certain vast bulk of the population of the red brick district of the lower West Side. Homeless, they have a hundred homes. They flit from furnished room to furnished room, transients forever—transients in abode, transients in heart and mind. They sing "Home, Sweet Home" in ragtime; they carry their lares et penates in a bandbox; their vine is entwined about a picture hat; a rubber plant is their fig tree.

Hence the houses of this district, having had a thousand dwellers, should have a thousand tales to tell, mostly dull ones, no doubt; but it would be strange if there could not be found a ghost or two in the wake of all these vagrant guests.

One evening after dark a young man prowled among these crumbling red mansions, ringing their bells. At the twelfth he rested his lean hand-baggage upon the step and wiped the dust from his hatband and forehead. The bell sounded faint and far away in some remote, hollow depths.

To the door of this, the twelfth house whose bell he had rung, came a housekeeper who made him think of an unwholesome, surfeited worm that had eaten its nut to a hollow shell and now sought to fill the vacancy with edible lodgers.

He asked if there was a room to let.

"Come in," said the housekeeper. Her voice came from her throat; her throat seemed lined with fur. "I have the third floor back, vacant since a week back. Should you wish to look at it?"

The young man followed her up the stairs. A faint light from no particular source mitigated the shadows of the halls.

居住在纽约下西区红砖房里的大部分人都行色仓皇，迁移不断、来去匆匆。他们无家可归，但也可以说有上百个家。他们不停地从这间带家具的出租屋搬到另一间，如随季节迁徙的候鸟一样永远居无定所，情感也无处可依，灵魂无处安放。他们和着拉格泰姆[①]的曲调唱着《甜蜜的家》；他们把拉列斯和珀那忒斯[②]两位家庭守护神放在纸盒里搬来搬去；葡萄藤只不过是绕在他们阔边帽上的装饰品；无花果树在他们看来也只不过是一株橡胶植物。[③]

在这里，有一千个租客，就有一千个故事。尽管大多数都乏善可陈，但如果说在这么多漂泊的躯壳里找不出一两个有故事的灵魂，那未免也太说不过去了。

有一天，夜幕降临以后，有个年轻男子在这些破烂不堪的红砖房中间来回穿梭，挨家挨户地按着门铃。当他走到第十二栋房子时，他把简单的手提行李放在台阶上，掸去帽檐上的土，抹掉额头上的灰。微弱的铃声从远处空荡的房屋深处传来。

这是他按响的第十二家门铃。门开了，出来一位女房东。那模样让他想起贪得无厌、暴饮暴食的蠕虫，仿佛刚把坚果吃得只剩下空壳，正等着房客来把它们填满。

年轻人问她是否有房间出租。

“进来吧，”房东用她那长满苔的鸭公嗓说道，“后面三楼还有个房间，上周才刚空出来。进来看看吧？”

年轻人跟着她上楼。不知何处透来的一丝微光，驱散了些许过道里的阴暗。他们悄无声息地爬着楼梯，脚下的地毯已破烂不堪，

① 拉格泰姆，ragtime，也称繁音拍子。美国流行音乐重要形式。由黑人旋律改编而成的早期爵士乐，盛行于第一次世界大战前后。
② （古罗马）诸家神，家庭守护神。
③ 《圣经·弥迦书》曾有载“人人都坐在自己的葡萄树下和无花果树下，不受惊吓。这是万军之主耶和华亲口说的。”此处葡萄藤和无花果树均为安居的象征。

They trod noiselessly upon a stair carpet that its own loom would have forsworn. It seemed to have become vegetable; to have degenerated in that rank, sunless air to lush lichen or spreading moss that grew in patches to the staircase and was viscid under the foot like organic matter. At each turn of the stairs were vacant niches in the wall. Perhaps plants had once been set within them. If so they had died in that foul and tainted air. It may be that statues of the saints had stood there, but it was not difficult to conceive that imps and devils had dragged them forth in the darkness and down to the unholy depths of some furnished pit below.

"This is the room," said the housekeeper, from her furry throat. "It's a nice room. It ain't often vacant. I had some most elegant people in it last summer—no trouble at all, and paid in advance to the minute. The water's at the end of the hall. Sprowls and Mooney kept it three months. They done a vaudeville sketch. Miss B'retta Sprowls—you may have heard of her—Oh, that was just the stage names—right there over the dresser is where the marriage certificate hung, framed. The gas is here, and you see there is plenty of closet room. It's a room everybody likes. It never stays idle long."

"Do you have many theatrical people rooming here?" asked the young man.

"They comes and goes. A good proportion of my lodgers is connected with the theatres. Yes, sir, this is the theatrical district. Actor people never stays long anywhere.

I get my share. Yes, they comes and they goes."

就连原先造出它的织布机都无法辨认出它了。那地毯仿佛变成了植物，在这腐臭阴暗的空气中，已退化成青翠繁茂的地衣和满地疯长的苔藓，一块块地铺满楼梯，踩上去黏糊糊的，仿佛踩到了鼻涕虫。楼梯拐角处的墙上是空着的壁龛，里面也许曾摆放过植物。但就算放过，那也早已在这恶臭污浊的空气中凋谢枯萎。里面也可能供奉过圣人的雕像，但不难想象，那些圣人也早已在黑暗中被那些无常小鬼、魑魅魍魉拉下，拖到带家具的地窖之下邪恶的深渊去了。

“就是这间，”房东继续用她那嘶哑的嗓子说，“房间非常好，几乎不会空出来。去年夏天这里还住过一些特别讲究的客人——他们从不惹麻烦，准时预付房租。水在走廊尽头。斯普罗尔斯和穆尼在这儿住过三个月，她们都是杂耍演员。布雷塔·斯普罗尔斯小姐——你可能听过她的芳名——不过，那只是她的艺名——就在那张梳妆台上方，原来还挂着她的结婚证，裱了框的。煤气在这儿，看这储物柜多宽敞。这样的房间人人都喜欢，从来不会空太久的。”

“您这儿住过很多戏剧演员吗？”年轻人问。

“房客们来来往往。他们大多数都与戏剧有关。不过，先生，这里是剧院区，演员们从不在一个地方长住。

在我这儿来住过的也不少。当然了，他们都是搬来搬去的。”

He engaged the room, paying for a week in advance. He was tired, he said, and would take possession at once. He counted out the money. The room had been made ready, she said, even to towels and water. As the housekeeper moved away he put, for the thousandth time, the question that he carried at the end of his tongue.

"A young girl—Miss Vashner—Miss Eloise Vashner—do you remember such a one among your lodgers? She would be singing on the stage, most likely. A fair girl, of medium height and slender, with reddish, gold hair and a dark mole near her left eyebrow."

"No, I don't remember the name. Them stage people has names they change as often as their rooms. They comes and they goes. No, I don't call that one to mind."

No. Always no. Five months of ceaseless interrogation and the inevitable negative. So much time spent by day in questioning managers, agents, schools and choruses; by night among the audiences of theatres from all-star casts down to music halls so low that he dreaded to find what he most hoped for. He who had loved her best had tried to find her. He was sure that since her disappearance from home this great, water-girt city held her somewhere, but it was like a monstrous quicksand, shifting its particles constantly, with no foundation, its upper granules of to-day buried to-morrow in ooze and slime.

The furnished room received its latest guest with a first glow of pseudo-hospitality, a hectic, haggard, perfunctory welcome like the specious smile of a demirep. The sophistical

年轻人定下那间房，预先支付了一周的租金。他说他很累，希望立马就能住下来。他付完租金后，女房东说房间早就备好了，连毛巾和水都准备了。房东正要离开时，他问起了那个他常挂在嘴边的问题，那个他问过一千次的问题。

“您是否记得房客中有一个叫瓦西纳的姑娘——埃洛伊丝·瓦西纳小姐？她可能是个歌唱演员。面容姣好，中等个子，身材苗条，泛红的金发，左边眉毛旁有颗黑痣。”

“没有，我不记得有这个名字。那些舞台上的演员们换名字跟换房间一样勤，换来换去的。我的确对这个名字没印象。”

没有。总是没有。五个月来无休止地打听询问，得到的回答都一模一样。数不清的日子里，那个年轻人白天去找剧院经理、经纪人、学校和合唱团打听；晚上从名角云集的剧院，到下三流的音乐厅，他都一个不落地去找过，他真害怕会在那些音乐厅找到他最想找的人。他深爱着她，拼尽全力想要找到她。他也深信，离家出走的她一定在这座四面环水的大城市的某个角落。但这座城市就像个巨大的流沙堆，沙粒的位置变化不定，没有固定的根基，今天还浮在上层的沙粒，也许明天就被埋进淤泥和黏土里。

这间带家具的出租屋看似热情地迎接着新房客，实则是在虚与委蛇、形容枯槁的脸上勉强挤出点儿笑容，像极了娼妓脸上虚伪的假笑。屋子里的家具破旧不堪；沙发和椅子表面的锦缎早已破破烂

comfort came in reflected gleams from the decayed furniture, the ragged brocade upholstery of a couch and two chairs, a footwide cheap pier glass between the two windows, from one or two gilt picture frames and a brass bedstead in a corner.

The guest reclined, inert, upon a chair, while the room, confused in speech as though it were an apartment in Babel, tried to discourse to him of its divers tenantry.

A polychromatic rug like some brilliant-flowered rectangular, tropical islet lay surrounded by a billowy sea of soiled matting. Upon the gay-papered wall were those pictures that pursue the homeless one from house to house—The Huguenot Lovers, The First Quarrel, The Wedding Breakfast, Psyche at the Fountain. The mantel's chastely severe outline was ingloriously veiled behind some pert drapery drawn rakishly askew like the sashes of the Amazonian ballet. Upon it was some desolate flotsam cast aside by the room's marooned when a lucky sail had borne them to a fresh port—a trifling vase or two, pictures of actresses, a medicine bottle, some stray cards out of a deck.

One by one, as the characters of a cryptograph become explicit, the little signs left by the furnished room's procession of guests developed a significance. The threadbare space in the rug in front of the dresser told that lovely woman had marched in the throng. Tiny finger prints on the wall spoke of little prisoners trying to feel their way to sun and air. A splattered stain, raying like the shadow of a bursting bomb, witnessed where a hurled glass or bottle had splintered with its contents against the wall. Across the pier glass had been scrawled with

烂；两扇窗户之间一英尺宽的廉价穿衣镜反射出微微的光亮；角落里还摆放着一两个镀金相框和一个铜制床架；所有这些都给人营造出一种舒适的假象。

新房客有气无力地躺在椅子上，而此时的房间就像巴比伦的通天塔[①]一样，正在用各种混杂的语言竭力讲述着过往房客的故事。

满是污渍的草席上铺了一张五颜六色的地毯，看上去像是波涛汹涌的大海围绕着一个鲜花灿烂的方形热带小岛。那鲜艳墙纸上的画作——《胡格诺情人》《第一次争吵》《婚礼早餐》《泉边的普赛克》——是无家可归的人从一间出租屋带到另一间出租屋的精神寄托。庄严清高的壁炉轮廓被一块满是褶皱的帘子遮得严严实实，帘子也挂得歪歪斜斜，就像南美芭蕾舞剧女演员身上的肩带。壁炉上面放着一些杂七杂八的东西——一两个廉价花瓶、女演员们的肖像、一个药瓶以及一些散落的扑克牌——大都是些曾困居于此的荒岛流浪者所遗弃之物，在幸运的船只将他们载到新码头时，他们随手把这些东西丢在了甲板上。

有如密码被逐个破译，先前房客留在房间里的蛛丝马迹渐渐有了清晰的意义。梳妆台前那片被磨光的地毯，表明曾有成群的漂亮女人在那里踩过。墙上小小的指印诉说着困居于此的孩子对墙外世界的渴望。一摊四溅开来的污渍，如同炸弹袭击后留下的痕迹，那是杯子或瓶子连同其中的液体一起被砸在墙上的证明。穿衣镜上被人用金刚石歪歪扭扭地刻着“玛丽”二字。似乎，这间屋子里的

① Babel，巴别塔。据《圣经·旧约·创世记》第11章记载，该塔为当时人类联合兴建的通往天堂的高塔。为了阻止人类的计划，上帝让人类说不同的语言，使人类相互之间不能沟通，该计划因此失败，人类自此各散东西。此处意为“多种语言混杂的说话声”，译为“通天塔”。

a diamond in staggering letters the name "Marie." It seemed that the succession of dwellers in the furnished room had turned in fury—perhaps tempted beyond forbearance by its garish coldness—and wreaked upon it their passions. The furniture was chipped and bruised; the couch, distorted by bursting springs, seemed a horrible monster that had been slain during the stress of some grotesque convulsion. Some more potent upheaval had cloven a great slice from the marble mantel. Each plank in the floor owned its particular cant and shriek as from a separate and individual agony. It seemed incredible that all this malice and injury had been wrought upon the room by those who had called it for a time their home; and yet it may have been the cheated home instinct surviving blindly, the resentful rage at false household gods that had kindled their wrath. A hut that is our own we can sweep and adorn and cherish.

The young tenant in the chair allowed these thoughts to file, soft-shod, through his mind, while there drifted into the room furnished sounds and furnished scents. He heard in one room a tittering and incontinent, slack laughter; in others the monologue of a scold, the rattling of dice, a lullaby, and one crying dully; above him a banjo tinkled with spirit. Doors banged somewhere; the elevated trains roared intermittently; a cat yowled miserably upon a back fence. And he breathed the breath of the house—a dank savour rather than a smell—a cold, musty effluvium as from underground vaults mingled with the reeking exhalations of linoleum and mildewed and rotten woodwork.

过往房客们——也许实在是无法忍受这客房内表面的俗丽与内在的冷漠——都把满腔怒火纷纷发泄在这里。家具满是伤痕：突起的弹簧使沙发变得像在痛苦的痉挛中被宰杀的恐怖怪物一样。大理石壁炉在某次激烈的闹剧里被撞掉了一大块。地上横七竖八的地板，因承受的痛苦各不相同，脚一踩上去，发出各种不同的吱呀乱叫，似乎在诉说着各自不同的哀怨。更令人难以置信的是，把所有恶意和伤害加诸这间房的人，竟是那些曾一度以此为家的人；不过，也许点燃他们心中熊熊怒火的，正是他们满以为可以逃避、实则根深蒂固却又无法满足的恋家本能，或是他们对虚假家神的愤恨。倘若那真是他们自己的家，哪怕只是一间茅草屋，他们都会仔细打扫、精心装饰并倍加珍惜。

椅子上的年轻房客任由这些思绪闯进大脑，在脑海中飘荡，掠过心头。与此同时，其他客房的声音与气味也都飘了进来。他听见有个房间传来狂野而慵懒且带着点儿神经质的笑声；还听见其他房间里传来滔滔不绝的咒骂声、摇骰子的格格声，还有催眠曲和低声哭泣的声音；楼上还有人将班卓琴[①]弹得激情洋溢。某个房门“砰”的一声关上了，轻轨列车呼啸而过，还有只猫在后院的篱笆上哀号。年轻房客闻到的满是这栋房子的气味儿——那不是臭气，而是一种潮湿的气味，就像是从地下室里翻腾上来的阴冷霉味，夹杂着油毡布和烂木头的味道。

① Banjo，班卓琴。上部形如吉他，下部形如铃鼓。该琴源于西非，于17世纪奴隶贸易时代被引入新大陆，在拓殖者中较为盛行。

Then, suddenly, as he rested there, the room was filled with the strong, sweet odour of mignonette. It came as upon a single buffet of wind with such sureness and fragrance and emphasis that it almost seemed a living visitant. And the man cried aloud: "What, dear?" as if he had been called, and sprang up and faced about. The rich odour clung to him and wrapped him around. He reached out his arms for it, all his senses for the time confused and commingled. How could one be peremptorily called by an odour? Surely it must have been a sound. But, was it not the sound that had touched, that had caressed him?

"She has been in this room," he cried, and he sprang to wrest from it a token, for he knew he would recognize the smallest thing that had belonged to her or that she had touched. This enveloping scent of mignonette, the odour that she had loved and made her own—whence came it?

The room had been but carelessly set in order. Scattered upon the flimsy dresser scarf were half a dozen hairpins—those discreet, indistinguishable friends of womankind, feminine of gender, infinite of mood and uncommunicative of tense.These he ignored, conscious of their triumphant lack of identity. Ransacking the drawers of the dresser he came upon a discarded, tiny, ragged handkerchief. He pressed it to his face. It was racy and insolent with heliotrope; he hurled it to the floor. In another drawer he found odd buttons, a theatre programme, a pawnbroker's card, two lost marshmallows, a book on the divination of dreams. In the last was a woman's black satin hair bow, which halted him, poised between ice and fire. But the

他躺在那儿，房间突然里泛起了木犀草的浓郁芳香。它随着一阵风扑鼻而来，清新浓烈，沁人心脾，好似一位鲜活的访客。年轻人喊了出来："什么？亲爱的？"仿佛有人在叫他似的。他一跃而起，四处张望。馥郁的香气萦绕在他身旁，包裹住了他。他伸出双臂想要触摸，但此时，他所有的感官都杂乱地搅在一起。香味怎么可能将人唤醒呢？那肯定是声音。可难道不是曾经触摸过、拥抱过他的声音吗？

"她在这个房间住过，"他大喊道，跳起来去找与她有关的蛛丝马迹，他确信，无论再微小的东西，只要是属于她或是她用过的，他都能准确地辨认出来。弥漫在这里的木犀花香，是她所喜爱的且属于她的气味——究竟从哪里来的呢？

房间只是简单地打扫过。梳妆台薄薄的桌布上散落着五六个发夹——发夹是女性的朋友，它们看起来不惹眼，模样相似，难以分辨，但那是女性日常所需。他没有留意这些发夹，因为他知道这些东西缺乏辨识度。他仔细搜寻了梳妆台抽屉的每个角落，发现了一条被丢弃的破烂的小手帕。他把它捂在脸上，闻到一股刺鼻的天芥菜花怪味，赶紧将它扔到地板上。在另一个抽屉里，他发现了几颗零星的纽扣，一张剧院节目单，一张当铺老板的名片，两颗被遗落的棉花糖，一本解梦的书。最后，他发现了一个女士的黑色缎面蝴蝶结。他愣住了，异常激动但又极力保持镇静。可黑缎蝴蝶结也不过是女性的普通饰品，也是没有个人特点的普通头饰而已，并不能说明什么。

black satin hairbow also is femininity's demure, impersonal, common ornament, and tells no tales.

And then he traversed the room like a hound on the scent, skimming the walls, considering the corners of the bulging matting on his hands and knees, rummaging mantel and tables, the curtains and hangings, the drunken cabinet in the corner, for a visible sign, unable to perceive that she was there beside, around, against, within, above him, clinging to him, wooing him, calling him so poignantly through the finer senses that even his grosser ones became cognisant of the call. Once again he answered loudly: "Yes, dear!" and turned, wild-eyed, to gaze on vacancy, for he could not yet discern form and colour and love and outstretched arms in the odour of mignonette. Oh, God! whence that odour, and since when have odours had a voice to call? Thus he groped.

He burrowed in crevices and corners, and found corks and cigarettes. These he passed in passive contempt. But once he found in a fold of the matting a half-smoked cigar, and this he ground beneath his heel with a green and trenchant oath. He sifted the room from end to end. He found dreary and ignoble small records of many a peripatetic tenant; but of her whom he sought, and who may have lodged there, and whose spirit seemed to hover there, he found no trace.

And then he thought of the housekeeper.

He ran from the haunted room downstairs and to a door that showed a crack of light. She came out to his knock. He smothered his excitement as best he could.

随后他像猎狗一样，寻着气味在房间里四处翻找，检查墙壁，趴在地上仔细查看凸起的地板，翻遍壁炉和桌子，查看窗帘和帷幔，搜寻角落里东倒西歪仿佛喝醉酒的小橱柜，竭力想找到一丝她留下的痕迹。但他却无法看见，她其实就在这里，在他旁边，占据了他身边的每个角落，围绕着他，面对着他，存于心中，记于脑海，紧紧地抱着他、追随着他，并通过敏锐的感觉凄苦地呼唤着他，哪怕他的感觉再迟钝，也能听见这声呼唤。他再次大声回答："我在这儿，亲爱的！"然后转身睁大双眼，凝视着空荡荡的房间，但他却无法从芬芳的木犀花香中辨别出形状、颜色、爱人和张开的双臂。老天爷啊，那芳香到底是从哪儿来的呢？又是从什么时候起香味开始具有呼唤之力？然后，他继续不断地寻找着。

他把房间里的裂缝和墙角都翻了个遍，只发现了些瓶塞和烟蒂。这些东西他轻瞟了一眼便不再理会。但当他在地上褶皱的垫子里找到半支雪茄时，他就用脚把它碾碎，然后铁青着脸狠狠地诅咒一番。他把整个房间里里外外仔仔细细地找了一遍，发现了许多漂泊在外的房客留下的枯燥乏味而又极不光彩的痕迹。但是，有关他正在找寻的她，可能曾在这里住过一段时间的她，专属的木犀草香还萦绕在此的她，他却未曾有丝毫发现。

就在这时，他想起了女房东。

他从怪事儿连连的房间跑下楼，来到露出一丝灯光的门前。听到他的敲门声，房东走了出来。他竭尽全力控制好自己的情绪。

"Will you tell me, madam," he besought her, "who occupied the room I have before I came?"

"Yes, sir. I can tell you again. 'Twas Sprowls and Mooney, as I said. Miss B'retta Sprowls it was in the theatres, but Missis Mooney she was. My house is well known for respectability. The marriage certificate hung, framed, on a nail over—"

"What kind of a lady was Miss Sprowls—in looks, I mean?"

Why, black-haired, sir, short, and stout, with a comical face. They left a week ago Tuesday."

"And before they occupied it?"

"Why, there was a single gentleman connected with the draying business. He left owing me a week. Before him was Missis Crowder and her two children, that stayed four months; and back of them was old Mr. Doyle, whose sons paid for him. He kept the room six months. That goes back a year, sir, and further I do not remember."

He thanked her and crept back to his room. The room was dead. The essence that had vivified it was gone. The perfume of mignonette had departed. In its place was the old, stale odour of mouldy house furniture, of atmosphere in storage.

The ebbing of his hope drained his faith. He sat staring at the yellow, singing gaslight. Soon he walked to the bed and began to tear the sheets into strips. With the blade of his knife he drove them tightly into every crevice around windows and door. When all was snug and taut he turned out the light, turned the gas full on again and laid himself gratefully upon the bed.

"夫人，您能告诉我，"他乞求道，"在我之前都有谁住过那个房间吗？"

"好的，先生。我可以再说一遍。我说过，是斯普罗尔斯和穆尼夫妇。布雷塔·斯普罗尔斯小姐是她在的艺名，其实她就是穆尼太太。都知道我的房子好。他们的结婚证还裱了框，挂在钉子上——"

"斯普罗尔斯小姐是怎样的人——我的意思是，她长什么样子？"

"她呀，先生，黑头发，矮矮胖胖，满脸滑稽。他们上周二就搬走了。"

"那在他们之前还有谁住过？"

"这个啊，是个单身汉，跑运输的。他还有一个星期的房租没给就跑了。在他以前是克劳德夫人和她两个孩子，他们住了四个月。再往前就是多伊尔老先生，房租是他儿子付的。他住了六个月。这都快说到一年前了，先生，再往前我可就不记得了。"

他向她道了谢，然后失魂落魄地慢慢挪回到房间。房间一片死寂。曾让这里生机盎然的东西都不见了，木犀草的香味也消失无踪，剩下的只是发霉的家具散发出来的老朽、陈腐的臭气。

希望如潮水般退去，信念也渐渐枯竭。他坐在那儿，呆呆地看着咝咝作响的黄色煤气灯。一会儿，他走到床边，把床单撕成条儿，然后用刀刃把这些布条紧紧塞进门窗周围的缝隙里。当一切都准备妥当后，他关掉灯，再次把煤气开到最大，心满意足地躺在床上。

It was Mrs. McCool's night to go with the can for beer. So she fetched it and sat with Mrs. Purdy in one of those subterranean retreats where house-keepers foregather and the worm dieth seldom.

"I rented out my third floor, back, this evening," said Mrs. Purdy, across a fine circle of foam. "A young man took it. He went up to bed two hours ago."

"Now, did ye, Mrs. Purdy, ma'am?" said Mrs. McCool, with intense admiration. "You do be a wonder for rentin' rooms of that kind. And did ye tell him, then?" she concluded in a husky whisper, laden with mystery.

"Rooms," said Mrs. Purdy, in her furriest tones, "are furnished for to rent. I did not tell him, Mrs. McCool."

"'Tis right ye are, ma'am; 'tis by renting rooms we kape alive. Ye have the rale sense for business, ma'am. There be many people will rayjict the rentin' of a room if they be tould a suicide has been after dyin' in the bed of it."

"As you say, we has our living to be making," remarked Mrs. Purdy.

"Yis, ma'am; 'tis true. 'Tis just one wake ago this day I helped ye lay out the third floor, back. A pretty slip of a colleen she was to be killin' herself wid the gas—a swate little face she had, Mrs. Purdy, ma'am."

"She'd a-been called handsome, as you say," said Mrs. Purdy, assenting but critical, "but for that mole she had a-growin' by her left eyebrow. Do fill up your glass again, Mrs. McCool."

今晚轮到麦库尔太太提着罐子去打啤酒了。她买酒回来后，和珀迪太太坐在地下室，那里是房东们聚会的地方，各种虫蚁肆虐。[①]

“今晚我把后面三楼的那间房租出去了，”珀迪太太隔着浓密的啤酒泡说道，“房客是个年轻小伙子。两小时以前他就睡了。”

“天哪，真有您的，珀迪太太，哦不，是夫人！”麦克库尔太太满脸崇拜地说着，“能把那种房子租出去，您真是太有才了。您告诉他那件事儿了吗？”她哑着嗓子神神秘秘地低声问道。

“房间，”珀迪太太用她那极度沙哑的嗓子说，“摆上家具就是为能租出去。我没跟他说那事儿，麦克库尔太太。”

“您说得对，夫人，我们都是靠收租为生的嘛。您的算盘可打得真精啊，夫人。他要知道这个房间里曾有人在床上自杀，肯定就不会租了。”

“就像你说的，我们也得生活啊。”珀迪太太说。

“是啊，夫人，这是实话。就在上周的今天，我帮您把后面三楼那间房子收拾出来的。多漂亮的小姑娘啊，竟然开煤气自尽——她那小脸蛋儿多好看啊，珀迪夫人，对吧。”

“不错，如你所说，她长得还算俊俏，”珀迪太太表示赞成，但仍不乏挑剔地说道，“只可惜，她左边眉毛边长了颗痣。再来一杯吧，麦克库尔太太。”

① the worm dieth seldom，虫子不会死的，出自《圣经》。《圣经·新约·马可福音》（9:48）：“在那里（指地狱），虫是不死的，火是不灭的。”在这里以“虫子不死”将房东们的聚会场所比作地狱。此处译为“各种虫蚁肆虐”。

The Ransom of Red Chief
红毛酋长的赎金

一个地势平坦的小镇，名字却叫“顶峰”。两个绑匪想靠绑架讹人钱财，却要自掏腰包才能把孩子送回去。绑架者以为能将孩子牢牢握在手心，却被孩子虐得体无完肤。被绑架的孩子不仅不哭不闹，反而和绑架者玩起了游戏，还拒不回家。孩子的父亲不但没有表现出一丝的担心着急，反而拒绝绑匪的赎金要求，还与绑匪讨价还价，最后还勒索了绑匪一把。满镇的居民明知孩子被绑架，非但没有四处寻找，反而表现出事不关己的优哉游哉。在《红毛酋长的赎金》中，欧·亨利不仅延续了他“欧·亨利式”的意外结局，更是在整个故事中构建了一连串的与众不同和意料之外：善良懦弱的绑匪，状况频出的肉票，不走寻常路的父亲，满镇子状况外的民众，共同上演了一起史无前例且非同寻常的绑架案。整个故事构思奇巧，情节简单而又曲折往复，各色人物栩栩如生，故事结尾又一如既往地“出人意料”。绑匪讹人钱财却“偷鸡不成蚀把米”，被绑架的孩子有违常理地欢快异常，走丢孩子的父亲没有痛心疾首，左邻右舍也不闻不问，这些都让人读来不免心生疑窦。到底是什么原因导致了整个故事的意料之外？是孩子打破“常规”的行为方式，还是人与人之间情感关系的疏离？在这个一连串“事与愿违”的故事背后，欧·亨利到底意欲向读者传递什么样的人生思考？是对“人性本恶”的嘲弄，还是对“人情温暖”的诉求？这一切的疑问，也许只有读过之后才能一探究竟。

IT LOOKED like a good thing: but wait till I tell you. We were down South, in Alabama—Bill Driscoll and myself—when this kidnapping idea struck us. It was, as Bill afterward expressed it, "during a moment of temporary mental apparition"; but we didn't find that out till later.

There was a town down there, as flat as a flannel-cake, and called Summit, of course. It contained inhabitants of as undeleterious and self-satisfied a class of peasantry as ever clustered around a Maypole.

Bill and me had a joint capital of about six hundred dollars, and we needed just two thousand dollars more to pull off a fraudulent town-lot scheme in Western Illinois with. We talked it over on the front steps of the hotel. Philoprogenitiveness, says we, is strong in semi-rural communities; therefore and for other reasons, a kidnapping project ought to do better there than in the radius of newspapers that send reporters out in plain clothes to stir up talk about such things. We knew that Summit couldn't get after us with anything stronger than constables and maybe some lackadaisical bloodhounds and a diatribe or two in the Weekly Farmers' Budget. So, it looked good.

We selected for our victim the only child of a prominent citizen named Ebenezer Dorset. The father was respectable and tight, a mortgage fancier and a stern, upright collection-plate passer and forecloser. The kid was a boy of ten, with bas-relief freckles, and hair the colour of the cover of the magazine you buy at the news-stand when you want to catch a train. Bill and me figured that Ebenezer would melt down for a ransom of two

这本应该是个好事儿：不过还是先听我讲完吧。我和比尔·德里斯科尔南下经过亚拉巴马州，这时脑海中突然出现了绑架的念头。后来，比尔说那是"一时的鬼迷心窍"，但当时的我们却并不这么想。

亚拉巴马州有个小镇，地势平坦得像一张煎饼，不过，小镇的名字却叫顶峰。镇上的居民每天过得都像是围着五朔节①花柱欢庆的农民一样，彼此和睦，且自得其乐。

比尔和我全身上下一共只有六百块，如果我们想在伊利诺伊州的西部地区买块黑市地，要实现这个计划，那至少还需要两千块。我们坐在旅馆前的台阶上想办法。依我们，城乡结合区的居民对孩子的宠爱肯定超乎寻常，而且跟那些附近有报社的地方相比，绑架在这里会更容易得手，这里不会出点事就派便衣记者去煽风点火。我们也清楚案发后顶峰镇可能会派几名警员，或许还有几条懒洋洋的警犬，再在《农民新闻周刊》上登出一两篇声讨文章，然而情况也仅限于此，他们不会花更多的精力在此事上。就当时我们的推理而言，那真是个绝妙的主意。

我们选择的绑架目标是小镇名人埃比尼泽·多尔斯特老爷家的独子。多尔斯特先生虽受人尊敬，但却十分吝啬；他对在教堂捐款讳莫如深，却钟情于抵押借款，且对依法取消回赎抵押品的规定欢迎之至。他儿子今年十岁，满脸浅浮雕似的雀斑，头发的颜色就跟你赶火车时在报摊上买的杂志封面一样。我和比尔都认为，埃比尼泽肯定会分文不差地交出两千块钱的赎金。不过事实如何，还是先

① Maypole，欧洲传统民间节日五朔节。用以祭祀树神、谷物神，庆祝农业收获及春天的来临。节庆期间，人们先去山林搬回一棵高大的无花果树或杉树，把枝叶和树下部的树皮除去，再用花草、花圈、彩旗和彩带装饰好，并将它竖立于空旷的场地。活动开始后，人们手拿与柱顶相连的彩带，围绕五月柱跳祭祀舞蹈以示庆祝，祈祷神灵保佑五谷丰登、子孙繁衍。

thousand dollars to a cent. But wait till I tell you.

About two miles from Summit was a little mountain, covered with a dense cedar brake. On the rear elevation of this mountain was a cave. There we stored provisions. One evening after sundown, we drove in a buggy past old Dorset's house. The kid was in the street, throwing rocks at a kitten on the opposite fence.

"Hey, little boy!" says Bill, "would you like to have a bag of candy and a nice ride?"

The boy catches Bill neatly in the eye with a piece of brick.

"That will cost the old man an extra five hundred dollars," says Bill, climbing over the wheel.

That boy put up a fight like a welter-weight cinnamon bear; but, at last, we got him down in the bottom of the buggy and drove away. We took him up to the cave and I hitched the horse in the cedar brake. After dark I drove the buggy to the little village, three miles away, where we had hired it, and walked back to the mountain.

Bill was pasting court-plaster over the scratches and bruises on his features. There was a burning behind the big rock at the entrance of the cave, and the boy was watching a pot of boiling coffee, with two buzzard tailfeathers stuck in his red hair. He points a stick at me when I come up, and says:

"Ha! cursed paleface, do you dare to enter the camp of Red Chief, the terror of the plains?"

"He's all right now," says Bill, rolling up his trousers and examining some bruises on his shins. "We're playing Indian.

听我讲完吧。

在距离顶峰镇约两英里的地方有座小山，山上长满了枝繁叶茂的杉树灌木。山后半山腰有个岩洞，我们把食物藏在里面。一天傍晚，太阳下山之后，我们驾着马车从老多尔斯特的家门前经过。他儿子正在大街上朝对面篱笆上的小猫扔石头。

“你好，小朋友！”比尔打着招呼。“想不想来袋儿糖果，坐马车到处逛逛啊？”

男孩向比尔扔来一块砖头，正中他的眼睛。

“这下你老头得多给五百块了。”比尔边说边爬下了车。

那孩子像一头半大的红棕熊一样奋力抵抗，但我们最终把他弄进了马车，飞驰离去。我们把他带到了山洞后，我又把马拴到一棵雪松上。天黑以后，我又驾车赶到三英里外的一个小村子将租来的马车还掉，再步行回山上。

比尔正往他满是抓痕和瘀伤的脸上涂抹鱼胶硬膏。洞口的大石头后面有一堆火，男孩正盯着火上一壶沸腾的咖啡，红色的头发上插着两根秃鹰尾巴上的羽毛。我一进来，他便用棍子指着我说：

“哈哈！你这该死的白脸鬼，竟敢闯入红毛酋长的地盘恐怖平原？”

“他终于消停点儿了，”比尔边说边卷起裤脚查看小腿上的伤，

We're making Buffalo Bill's show look like magic-lantern views of Palestine in the town hall. I'm Old Hank, the Trapper, Red Chief's captive, and I'm to be scalped at daybreak. By Geronimo! that kid can kick hard."

Yes, sir, that boy seemed to be having the time of his life. The fun of camping out in a cave had made him forget that he was a captive, himself. He immediately christened me Snake-eye, the Spy, and announced that, when his braves returned from the warpath, I was to be broiled at the stake at the rising of the sun.

Then we had supper; and he filled his mouth full of bacon and bread and gravy, and began to talk. He made a during-dinner speech something like this:

"I like this fine. I never camped out before; but I had a pet 'possum once, and I was nine last birthday. I hate to go to school. Rats ate up sixteen of Jimmy Talbot's aunt's speckled hen's eggs. Are there any real Indians in these woods? I want some more gravy. Does the trees moving make the wind blow? We had five puppies. What makes your nose so red, Hank? My father has lots of money. Are the stars hot? I whipped Ed Walker twice, Saturday. I don't like girls. You dassent catch toads unless with a string. Do oxen make any noise? Why are oranges round? Have you got beds to sleep on in this cave? Amos Murray has got Six toes. A parrot can talk, but a monkey or a fish can't. How many does it take to make twelve?"

Every few minutes he would remember that he was a pesky redskin, and pick up his stick rifle and tiptoe to the mouth of the cave to rubber for the scouts of the hated paleface. Now

“我们在玩印第安人游戏。和我们比起来，野牛比尔[①]的表演就像是镇上影院里播放的巴勒斯坦幻灯片一样无趣。我演老汉克，是个猎人，也是红毛酋长的俘虏，明天破晓我就要被剥头皮了。杰罗尼莫[②]，那小孩踢人可疼了！”

的确，先生，那孩子似乎正处于他人生中最开心的一段日子。在山洞里露营的乐趣使他忘了自己是个肉票。他甚至还给我取名叫“蛇眼”，是一名探子，并宣称等他的印第安勇士征战归来后，他们会在日出之时把我绑在火刑柱上烧死。

紧接着，我们吃晚饭了。他嘴里塞满了熏肉、面包和酱汁，但仍在喋喋不休地说着。他的席间演讲内容大致如下：

“我太高兴了。我之前从未露营过，但我曾经养过一只小负鼠当宠物。我刚给自己过完九岁生日。我讨厌上学。吉米·塔尔博特的姨妈家养的花斑老母鸡下的蛋，被老鼠偷吃了十六个。这片森林里真有印第安人吗？给我再来点儿酱汁。刮风是因为树在动吗？我们家有五只小狗。汉克，你的鼻子为什么这么红？我爸爸超有钱。天上的星星是热的吗？星期六我揍了埃德·沃克两次。我不喜欢女孩子。没有绳子你就捉不到癞蛤蟆。公牛会乱叫吗？橙子为什么是圆的？你们山洞里有床吗？阿莫斯·默里长了六个脚趾。鹦鹉会说话，但猴子和鱼都不会。几乘几等于十二？”

每隔几分钟，他就会记起自己是个令人生厌的印第安人，拿起他那根棍子当枪使，蹑手蹑脚地走到洞口去观察，看看有没有烦人

① Buffalo Bill，野牛比尔，威廉·弗雷德里克·科迪（Buffalo Bill Cody，1846–1917），水牛猎人、美军侦察兵及印第安战士。美国蛮荒西部的代表人物，曾制作过一场名为《野牛比尔的西大荒及世界级驯马师大会》（Buffalo Bill's Wild West and Congress of Rough Riders of the World）的话剧，该剧塑造了享誉全球的美国西部人物形象。老汉克和红酋长均为该剧中人物。

② Geronimo，杰罗尼莫（1829–1909），美国西南部阿帕切印第安人领袖。他曾领导阿帕切印第安人抗击美洲欧人入侵，具有超强的求生技能。此处应指文中的“山姆”，符合他在整个绑架案中的领导者身份。

and then he would let out a war-whoop that made Old Hank the Trapper shiver. That boy had Bill terrorized from the start.

"Red Chief," says I to the kid, "would you like to go home?"

"Aw, what for?" says he. "I don't have any fun at home. I hate to go to school. I like to camp out. You won't take me back home again, Snake-eye, will you?"

"Not right away," says I. "We'll stay here in the cave a while."

"All right!" says he. "That'll be fine. I never had such fun in all my life."

We went to bed about eleven o'clock. We spread down some wide blankets and quilts and put Red Chief between us. We weren't afraid he'd run away. He kept us awake for three hours, jumping up and reaching for his rifle and screeching: "Hist! pard," in mine and Bill's ears, as the fancied crackle of a twig or the rustle of a leaf revealed to his young imagination the stealthy approach of the outlaw band. At last, I fell into a troubled sleep, and dreamed that I had been kidnapped and chained to a tree by a ferocious pirate with red hair.

Just at daybreak, I was awakened by a series of awful screams from Bill. They weren't yells, or howls, or shouts, or whoops, or yawps, such as you'd expect from a manly set of vocal organs—they were simply indecent, terrifying, humiliating screams, such as women emit when they see ghosts or caterpillars. It's an awful thing to hear a strong, desperate, fat man scream incontinently in a cave at daybreak.

I jumped up to see what the matter was. Red Chief was

的白人探子。他偶尔还发出一声战斗呐喊。那喊声让俘虏老汉克直哆嗦。那小孩从一开始就把比尔吓得不轻。

"红毛酋长，"我对小孩说，"你想回家吗？"

"哦，回家干吗？"他说，"在家一点都不好玩。我讨厌上学。我喜欢露营。蛇眼，你不会送我回去的，对吧？"

"暂时不会，"我说，"我们要在这个山洞里待上一阵子。"

"好啊！"他说。"真是太好了。我从来没有这样开心地玩过。"

我们大约十一点去睡觉。我们铺了几条宽毛毯和被子，把红毛酋长放在我们中间。我们不担心他会逃跑，但他却让我们三个小时都没合眼。树枝断裂声和树叶沙沙声在他那小脑袋里都能被想象为有歹徒在悄悄靠近，于是他时不时地跳起身，伸手去拿他的那杆"长枪"，还在我和比尔的耳边不停地说："嘘，豹子来了！"终于，我睡着了，一点儿都不安稳，还梦见自己被一个凶残的红发海盗绑架了，用链子捆在了树上。

天刚一亮，我就被比尔一连串可怕的尖叫声惊醒了。那声音不是叫，不是喊，不是嚷，也不是吼，更不是咆哮，完全不像从男性发音器官里发出的；那是不堪入耳，让人毛骨悚然而又倍感难堪的尖叫声，就像女人见到鬼或毛毛虫时发出的尖叫一样。在拂晓时分的山洞里听见一个强壮而绝望的胖子无法自制的尖叫声，实在是非常糟心。

我跳起来想一探究竟。发现红毛酋长正骑在比尔的胸口，一只

sitting on Bill's chest, with one hand twined in Bill's hair. In the other he had the sharp case-knife we used for slicing bacon; and he was industriously and realistically trying to take Bill's scalp, according to the sentence that had been pronounced upon him the evening before.

I got the knife away from the kid and made him lie down again. But, from that moment, Bill's spirit was broken. He laid down on his side of the bed, but he never closed an eye again in sleep as long as that boy was with us. I dozed off for a while, but along toward sun-up I remembered that Red Chief had said I was to be burned at the stake at the rising of the sun. I wasn't nervous or afraid; but I sat up and lit my pipe and leaned against a rock.

"What you getting up so soon for, Sam?" asked Bill.

"Me?" says I. "Oh, I got a kind of a pain in my shoulder. I thought sitting up would rest it."

"You're a liar!" says Bill. "You're afraid. You was to be burned at sunrise, and you was afraid he'd do it. And he would, too, if he could find a match. Ain't it awful, Sam? Do you think anybody will pay out money to get a little imp like that back home?"

"Sure," said I. "A rowdy kid like that is just the kind that parents dote on. Now, you and the Chief get up and cook breakfast, while I go up on the top of this mountain and reconnoitre."

I went up on the peak of the little mountain and ran my eye over the contiguous vicinity. Over toward Summit I expected to see the sturdy yeomanry of the village armed with scythes and

手拽着比尔的头发，另一只手拿着我们切熏肉的锋利餐刀。根据前一晚红毛酋长对比尔的宣判，他正在比画要怎样剥下他的头皮。

我夺下孩子手中的刀，让他回去接着睡觉。但从那一刻起，比尔就一直惊魂不定。他虽然躺在床上，但只要那个孩子与我们在一起，他就一直不敢睡觉。我倒是眯了一会儿。快要日出时，我突然想起来红毛酋长说过要在日出时把我绑在火刑柱上烧死。我并不紧张，也不害怕，但我坐了起来，点上烟斗，斜靠在一块石头上。

“你怎么这么早就起来了，山姆？”比尔问。

“我？”我说。“噢，我一边的肩膀有点痛。我想坐着会舒服点儿。”

“鬼扯！”比尔说。“你害怕了。你被判天亮时火刑，你害怕他真把你烧了。只要他能找到哪怕一根火柴，他肯定会烧你。山姆，你不觉得那孩子很可怕吗？就这么个捣蛋鬼，谁肯花钱把他赎回家呀？”

“当然会有，”我说，“父母最宠爱这样淘气的孩子。现在，你和酋长起来做早饭，我去山顶看看。”

我爬上山顶，环顾四周。我原以为朝向顶峰镇的方向，会有很多强壮的村民拿着镰刀和草叉四处搜寻卑鄙的绑匪。但眼前却如同风景画一样宁静，只有一个人牵着头褐色骡子在犁地。小溪里无

pitchforks beating the countryside for the dastardly kidnappers. But what I saw was a peaceful landscape dotted with one man ploughing with a dun mule. Nobody was dragging the creek; no couriers dashed hither and yon, bringing tidings of no news to the distracted parents. There was a sylvan attitude of somnolent sleepiness pervading that section of the external outward surface of Alabama that lay exposed to my view. "Perhaps," says I to myself, "it has not yet been discovered that the wolves have home away the tender lambkin from the fold. Heaven help the wolves!" says I, and I went down the mountain to breakfast.

When I got to the cave I found Bill backed up against the side of it, breathing hard, and the boy threatening to smash him with a rock half as big as a cocoanut.

"He put a red-hot boiled potato down my back," explained Bill, "and then mashed it with his foot; and I boxed his ears. Have you got a gun about you, Sam?

I took the rock away from the boy and kind of patched up the argument. "I'll fix you," says the kid to Bill. "No man ever yet struck the Red Chief but what he got paid for it. You better beware!"

After breakfast the kid takes a piece of leather with strings wrapped around it out of his pocket and goes outside the cave unwinding it.

"What's he up to now?" says Bill, anxiously. "You don't think he'll run away, do you, Sam?"

"No fear of it," says I. "He don't seem to be much of a home body. But we've got to fix up some plan about the ransom.

人打捞；也没人四处奔走，告诉他的父母，孩子仍杳无音讯。眼前的阿拉巴马如森林般弥漫着朦胧的睡意。“也许，”我自言自语，“他们还没发现羊圈中的羊羔被狼叼走了。保佑狼吧！”说完，我便下山吃饭。

我到达山洞时，发现比尔正背靠着一侧的洞壁，呼吸急促，而那孩子正拿着半个椰子大的石头威胁说要把他砸得稀烂。

“他把一个滚烫的土豆从衣领塞进了我的后背，”比尔解释道，“还用脚把土豆给踩碎了；我就打了他一耳光。山姆，你身上带枪了吗？”

我夺过男孩手里的石头，平息了这场闹剧。“看我不揍你，”男孩对比尔说，“打了红毛酋长，还想不受罚，你给我等着。”

早饭后，那孩子从兜里掏出一块用绳子缠着的皮革，边解绳子边往洞外走。

“他又要干吗？”比尔焦虑地说，“你说他不会是要逃跑吧，山姆？”

“别担心，”我说，“他不像是个恋家的孩子。不过我们需要调整一下拿赎金的计划。他去了，顶峰镇至今还没有什么动静；不过

There don't seem to be much excitement around Summit on account of his disappearance; but maybe they haven't realized yet that he's gone. His folks may think he's spending the night with Aunt Jane or one of the neighbours. Anyhow, he'll be missed to-day. To-night we must get a message to his father demanding the two thousand dollars for his return."

Just then we heard a kind of war-whoop, such as David might have emitted when he knocked out the champion Goliath. It was a sling that Red Chief had pulled out of his pocket, and he was whirling it around his head.

I dodged, and heard a heavy thud and a kind of a sigh from Bill, like a horse gives out when you take his saddle off. A niggerhead rock the size of an egg had caught Bill just behind his left ear. He loosened himself all over and fell in the fire across the frying pan of hot water for washing the dishes. I dragged him out and poured cold water on his head for half an hour.

By and by, Bill sits up and feels behind his ear and says: "Sam, do you know who my favourite Biblical character is?"

"Take it easy," says I. "You'll come to your senses presently."

"King Herod," says he. "You won't go away and leave me here alone, will you, Sam?"

I went out and caught that boy and shook him until his freckles rattled.

"If you don't behave," says I, "I'll take you straight home. Now, are you going to be good, or not?"

"I was only funning," says he sullenly. "I didn't mean to hurt Old Hank. But what did he hit me for? I'll behave, Snake-

也许他们还没发现他不见了。他家人可能还以为他昨晚在珍妮姨妈家或哪个邻居家过夜呢。不管怎样，他们今天肯定会发现的。今晚，我们必须给他父亲捎个口信，拿两千块赎这小子回家。"

就在这时，我们听到一声印第安人宣战时的呐喊，那声音如同大卫当年用石块将勇士歌利亚[①]击倒时发出的声音。原来红毛酋长刚才从兜里掏出来的是个投石环，此刻他正从头顶飞快地甩着那武器。

我急忙闪开，随后听见砰的一声重响，接着就听见比尔的呻吟声，就像是马被卸下马鞍后发出的声音一样。一块鸡蛋大小的黑色石头恰好打中了比尔的左耳后根，他晕了过去，横倒在火堆上烧着洗碗水的热锅上。我把他拖到一边，往他头上浇了半个小时的冷水。

渐渐地，比尔坐了起来，摸着耳后根说："山姆，你知道我最喜欢《圣经》中的谁吗？"

"别着急，"我说，"你马上就会清醒了。"

"希律王，"[②]他说，"你不会丢下我，自己跑了吧，山姆？"

我走出去抓住那孩子一阵猛摇，晃到他脸上的雀斑都快掉下来。

"你要是再不听话，"我说，"我就直接把你送回家。现在，你是乖乖听话，还是继续胡闹？"

"我不过是闹着玩的，"他一脸不高兴地说，"我不是有意要伤害

① 歌利亚，Goliath，希伯来神话中的著名巨人之一。据《圣经》记载，歌利亚是非利士将军，曾带兵进攻以色列军队，力大无穷，让所有人看到他都退避三舍。牧童大卫投石弹打中歌利亚的脑袋，并割下其首级。大卫后来统一以色列，成为著名的大卫王。

② 希律王，King Herod，《圣经·新约》中人物，为耶稣诞生时期的犹太王。据《圣经·新约·马太福音》第二章记载，有人预言耶稣将会成为犹太王，希律王唯恐预言应验，下令将伯利恒及其周围境内两岁及以下的所有婴儿杀死。

eye, if you won't send me home, and if you'll let me play the Black Scout to-day."

"I don't know the game," says I. "That's for you and Mr. Bill to decide. He's your playmate for the day. I'm going away for a while, on business. Now, you come in and make friends with him and say you are sorry for hurting him, or home you go, at once."

I made him and Bill shake hands, and then I took Bill aside and told him I was going to Poplar Cove, a little village three miles from the cave, and find out what I could about how the kidnapping had been regarded in Summit. Also, I thought it best to send a peremptory letter to old man Dorset that day, demanding the ransom and dictating how it should be paid.

"You know, Sam," says Bill, "I've stood by you without batting an eye in earthquakes, fire and flood—in poker games, dynamite outrages, police raids, train robberies and cyclones. I never lost my nerve yet till we kidnapped that two-legged skyrocket of a kid. He's got me going. You won't leave me long with him, will you, Sam?"

"I'll be back some time this afternoon," says I. "You must keep the boy amused and quiet till I return. And now we'll write the letter to old Dorset."

Bill and I got paper and pencil and worked on the letter while Red Chief, with a blanket wrapped around him, strutted up and down, guarding the mouth of the cave. Bill begged me tearfully to make the ransom fifteen hundred dollars instead of two thousand. "I ain't attempting," says he, "to decry the celebrated moral aspect of parental affection, but we're dealing

老汉克。可他凭什么打我呀？蛇眼，只要你不赶我走，而且今天就让我玩黑人侦察游戏，那我一定听话。”

“我不会玩这个游戏，”我说，“你去问问比尔先生会不会。今天他陪你玩，我有事要出去一趟。现在，你进去跟他讲和，向他道歉，否则立刻让你回家。”

我让他跟比尔罢手言和。之后我将比尔拉到一旁，告诉他我要去离山洞三英里远的一个名叫杨树湾的小村庄打听消息，看看顶峰镇的人们对这起绑架案有什么反应。而且，我们最好今天就给老多尔斯特先生送一封态度强硬的信，直接写上要多少赎金，并告知他交款的时间和地点。

“你知道，山姆，”比尔说，“无论情况多么危急，我都会和你站在一起，眼睛都不眨一下，不管是玩牌、丢炸弹，还是袭警、抢火车。要不是绑了这个两条腿的冲天炮[①]，我还真不知道什么叫害怕。他快把我折腾疯了。你不会让我一个人陪他很久的，对吧，山姆？”

“我下午就回来，”我说，“你先陪他好好玩，等我回来。现在，我们来给老多尔斯特写信。”

我们拿出纸和笔开始写信，而红毛酋长此时正裹着毯子，上蹿下跳，大摇大摆地在洞口来回巡视。比尔含泪求我把赎金改为一千五百。“我并不是，”他说，“要贬低世人称颂的神圣父母之爱，但我们这是在与人打交道，是人都不会为了买一只四十磅重的花脸

① skyrocket，流星烟火、冲天火箭。此处形容小孩咋咋呼呼，惡作剧嚣张。故译为“冲天炮”。

with humans, and it ain't human for anybody to give up two thousand dollars for that forty-pound chunk of freckled wildcat. I'm willing to take a chance at fifteen hundred dollars. You can charge the difference up to me."

So, to relieve Bill, I acceded, and we collaborated a letter that ran this way:

Ebenezer Dorset, Esq.:

We have your boy concealed in a place far from Summit. It is useless for you or the most skilful detectives to attempt to find him. Absolutely, the only terms on which you can have him restored to you are these: We demand fifteen hundred dollars in large bills for his return; the money to be left at midnight tonight at the same spot and in the same box as your reply—as hereinafter described. If you agree to these terms, send your answer in writing by a solitary messenger to-night at half-past eight o'clock. After crossing Owl Creek, on the road to Poplar Cove, there are three large trees about a hundred yards apart, close to the fence of the wheat field on the right-hand side. At the bottom of the fence-post, opposite the third tree, will be found a small pasteboard box.

The messenger will place the answer in this box and return immediately to Summit.

If you attempt any treachery or fail to comply with our demand as stated, you will never see your boy again.

If you pay the money as demanded, he will be returned to you safe and well within three hours. These terms are final, and

猫花上两千块的。我宁愿少要五百块。你可以把这笔差额记在我的账上。”

为了让比尔安心，我同意了。于是我们俩商量着写了这样一封信：

尊敬的埃比尼泽·多尔斯特先生：

您儿子已经被我们藏在了离顶峰镇很远的地方。无论是您本人还是任何神探都不可能找到他，所以别白费力气了。想要回儿子，就得答应这些条款：我们要一千五百块的大面额钞票作为赎金；付款方式与回信方式相同，今天午夜放至同一地点的同一盒子里。如同意上述条件，请以书信形式回复，今晚八点半派人单独送来。在穿过枭河去杨树湾的路上，路右边离麦田篱笆一百码左右的地方有三棵大树，第三棵树对面的篱笆桩底下有个小纸盒。

送信人将回信放入盒子后必须立马返回顶峰镇。

如果您敢耍花招或拒不答应上述条件，您就永远别想见到您的儿子。

只要您按要求交款，您的儿子将在三个小时之内毫发无损地回到您身边。此事没得商量，其他任何条件，一概免谈。

两个亡命徒

if you do not accede to them no further communication will be attempted.

TWO DESPERATE MEN

I addressed this letter to Dorset, and put it in my pocket. As I was about to start, the kid comes up to me and says:

"Aw, Snake-eye, you said I could play the Black Scout while you was gone."

"Play it, of course," says I. "Mr. Bill will play with you. What kind of a game is it?"

"I'm the Black Scout," says Red Chief, "and I have to ride to the stockade to warn the settlers that the Indians are coming. I'm tired of playing Indian myself. I want to be the Black Scout."

"All right," says I. "It sounds harmless to me. I guess Mr. Bill will help you foil the pesky savages."

"What am I to do?" asks Bill, looking at the kid suspiciously.

"You are the hoss," says Black Scout. "Get down on your hands and knees. How can I ride to the stockade without a hoss?"

"You'd better keep him interested," said I, "till we get the scheme going. Loosen up."

Bill gets down on his all fours, and a look comes in his eye like a rabbit's when you catch it in a trap.

"How far is it to the stockade, kid?" he asks, in a husky manner of voice.

我在信封上写下多尔斯特的地址，将信放进口袋。正要出发，男孩朝我走来，说：

“喂，蛇眼，你答应过我，你走了以后我可以玩黑人侦察兵游戏的。”

“玩吧，当然可以。”我说。“比尔先生会陪你玩。那是个什么游戏？”

“我是黑人侦察兵”，红毛酋长说，“我要骑马去寨子里，告诉乡民印第安人来了。我不想再扮演印第安人了。我想当黑人侦察兵。”

“当然可以，”我说，“你想扮谁都可以。比尔先生肯定会帮你击退那些讨厌的家伙。”

“那我要做什么呢？”比尔一脸迟疑地看着小孩问道。

“你当马，”黑人侦察兵说，“要跪着，用手和膝盖撑在地上爬。我没有马怎么去寨子呢？”

“你可得陪他好好玩，”我说，“直到我们的计划有所进展。放轻松点。”

比尔四肢着地，如同陷阱里的兔子一样，满眼绝望。

“到寨子有多远，小子？”他用沙哑的声音问道。

"Ninety miles," says the Black Scout. "And you have to hump yourself to get there on time. Whoa, now!"

The Black Scout jumps on Bill's back and digs his heels in his side.

"For Heaven's sake," says Bill, "hurry back, Sam, as soon as you can. I wish we hadn't made the ransom more than a thousand. Say, you quit kicking me or I'll get up and warm you good."

I walked over to Poplar Cove and sat around the post-office and store, talking with the chawbacons that came in to trade. One whiskerand says that he hears Summit is all upset on account of Elder Ebenezer Dorset's boy having been lost or stolen. That was all I wanted to know. I bought some smoking tobacco, referred casually to the price of black-eyed peas, posted my letter surreptitiously and came away. The postmaster said the mail-carrier would come by in an hour to take the mail on to Summit.

When I got back to the cave Bill and the boy were not to be found. I explored the vicinity of the cave, and risked a yodel or two, but there was no response.

So I lighted my pipe and sat down on a mossy bank to await developments.

In about half an hour I heard the bushes rustle, and Bill wabbled out into the little glade in front of the cave. Behind him was the kid, stepping softly like a scout, with a broad grin on his face. Bill stopped, took off his hat and wiped his face with a red handkerchief. The kid stopped about eight feet behind him.

“九十英里，”黑人侦察兵说，“你必须竭尽全力准时赶到那里。驾！出发！”

黑人侦察兵跳到比尔背上，双脚在比尔肋骨上蹬了一下。

“看在上帝的分上，”比尔说，“你快去快回，山姆。我们真不该把赎金定在一千以上。小子，你再踢我，我就起来揍你。”

我走到杨树湾，在那家充当邮局的杂货店里坐下，与进店买东西的乡民们闲聊。有个满脸胡子的人说，现在整个顶峰镇愁云密布，因为埃比尼泽·多尔斯特的儿子不知是走丢了还是被人拐走了。这正是我想打听的。我买了些烟丝，随口问了问豇豆的价格，离开时偷偷将信塞进了邮箱。听邮局负责人说，邮差一个小时之内就会过来取件，然后送往顶峰镇。

我回到山洞时，比尔和孩子都不见了。我在附近找了一圈儿，还冒险大喊了两声，但都不见回应。

我只好点起烟斗，坐在长满青草的斜坡上慢慢等。

约莫过了半小时，灌木丛里传来沙沙的响声，随后比尔从里面摇摇晃晃地出来，走到山洞前的空地上。男孩跟在后面，蹑手蹑脚地像个侦探，咧着嘴笑。比尔停下来，摘掉帽子，用块红手帕擦了擦汗。那孩子就一动不动地站在他身后大约八英尺远的地方。

"Sam," says Bill, "I suppose you'll think I'm a renegade, but I couldn't help it. I'm a grown person with masculine proclivities and habits of self-defense, but there is a time when all systems of egotism and predominance fail. The boy is gone. I have sent him home. All is off. There was martyrs in old times," goes on Bill, "that suffered death rather than give up the particular graft they enjoyed. None of 'em ever was subjugated to such supernatural tortures as I have been. I tried to be faithful to our articles of depredation; but there came a limit."

"What's the trouble, Bill?" I asks him.

"I was rode," says Bill, "the ninety miles to the stockade, not barring an inch. Then, when the settlers was rescued, I was given oats. Sand ain't a palatable substitute. And then, for an hour I had to try to explain to him why there was nothin' in holes, how a road can run both ways and what makes the grass green. I tell you, Sam, a human can only stand so much. I takes him by the neck of his clothes and drags him down the mountain. On the way he kicks my legs black-and-blue from the knees down; and I've got to have two or three bites on my thumb and hand cauterized.

"But he's gone"— continues Bill —"gone home. I showed him the road to Summit and kicked him about eight feet nearer there at one kick. I'm sorry we lose the ransom; but it was either that or Bill Driscoll to the madhouse."

Bill is puffing and blowing, but there is a look of ineffable peace and growing content on his rose-pink features.

"Bill," says I, "there isn't any heart disease in your family,

“山姆，”比尔说，“你可能会觉得我背信弃义，但我实在受不了。我是个成年人，有男子汉的气魄和正当防卫能力，但也有自尊与骄傲通通被摧毁的时候。那孩子已经走了，我把他送回家了。一切都结束了。古时候有殉道者，”比尔接着说，“他们宁死也不愿改变初衷继续苟活。但他们没有一个人像我这样受过这种非人的折磨。我也想尽全力把钱拿到手再说，但我实在是受不了了。”

“怎么了，比尔？”我问。

“我驮着他，”比尔说，“一英寸都不带少的，走了九十英里到达那个寨子。寨子里的人倒是得救了，但他却把沙子当燕麦喂给我吃。随后的一个小时里，我不得不给他解释，为什么山洞里什么都没有，为什么一条路的两个方向都能走，草为什么是绿色的。我敢说，山姆，一个人就只能承受这么多。我拽着他的衣领，把他拖下了山。一路上我的小腿被他踢得青一块紫一块；大拇指也被他咬了两三口，整只手都火辣辣地疼。”

“还好他已经走了，”比尔继续说，“回家了。我把去顶峰镇的路指给他看，一脚把他踢出八英尺远。对不起，我们的赎金没了，但如果不这样，比尔·德里斯科尔肯定会疯的。”

比尔说得呼吸急促，不停喘气，但他那红红的脸上却有着无法言说的平静与慢慢恢复的安然。

“比尔，”我问，“你们家族没有心脏病史吧？”

is there?

"No," says Bill, "nothing chronic except malaria and accidents. Why?"

"Then you might turn around," says I, "and have a took behind you."

Bill turns and sees the boy, and loses his complexion and sits down plump on the round and begins to pluck aimlessly at grass and little sticks. For an hour I was afraid for his mind. And then I told him that my scheme was to put the whole job through immediately and that we would get the ransom and be off with it by midnight if old Dorset fell in with our proposition. So Bill braced up enough to give the kid a weak sort of a smile and a promise to play the Russian in a Japanese war with him is soon as he felt a little better.

I had a scheme for collecting that ransom without danger of being caught by counterplots that ought to commend itself to professional kidnappers. The tree under which the answer was to be left—and the money later on—was close to the road fence with big, bare fields on all sides. If a gang of constables should be watching for any one to come for the note they could see him a long way off crossing the fields or in the road. But no, sirree! At half-past eight I was up in that tree as well hidden as a tree toad, waiting for the messenger to arrive.

Exactly on time, a half-grown boy rides up the road on a bicycle, locates the pasteboard box at the foot of the fence-post, slips a folded piece of paper into it and pedals away again back toward Summit.

“没有，”比尔说道，“除了疟疾和意外，没人得慢性病。为什么这么问？”

“那你可以转过身，”我说，“看看你身后是谁。”

比尔一转身就看到了那孩子，他惊慌失措地扑通一声瘫坐在地上，抓狂地拽着草和小树枝。在接下来的一个小时，我都在担心，怕他精神崩溃。后来，我告诉他，我的计划是尽快了结这件事；如果老多尔斯特答应我们的条件，我们拿到赎金就连夜离开。听到这儿，比尔才重新振作，给孩子挤出一丝苦笑，并答应孩子，等身体感觉稍微好点后就陪他玩俄国人打日本人的游戏。

我有个取回赎金的好主意，不存在落入圈套被抓的危险，应该把它推荐给职业绑架者。那棵大树——就是要放赎金的那棵大树——离路边的篱笆很近，篱笆墙内是一大片光秃秃的田野。如果有警察在那儿蹲守，他们在取信人穿过田野或公路，还离得很远的时候就能发现他。但我也不傻呀，先生！我八点半之前就爬上了树，像只树蛙一样把自己藏得严严实实，只等送信人来。

对方倒还准时，一个半大小伙儿骑着自行车来了。他在篱笆桩下找到了纸盒，塞了张纸进去，随即踩着自行车又回顶峰镇去了。

I waited an hour and then concluded the thing was square. I slid down the tree, got the note, slipped along the fence till I struck the woods, and was back at the cave in another half an hour. I opened the note, got near the lantern and read it to Bill. It was written with a pen in a crabbed hand, and the sum and substance of it was this:

Two Desperate Men,

Gentlemen:

I received your letter to-day by post, in regard to the ransom you ask for the return of my son. I think you are a little high in your demands, and I hereby make you a counter-proposition, which I am inclined to believe you will accept. You bring Johnny home and pay me two hundred and fifty dollars in cash, and I agree to take him off your hands. You had better come at night, for the neighbours believe he is lost, and I couldn't be responsible for what they would do to anybody they saw bringing him back.

Very respectfully,

EBENEZER DORSET

"Great pirates of Penzance!" says I; "of all the impudent—"

But I glanced at Bill, and hesitated. He had the most appealing look in his eyes I ever saw on the face of a dumb or a talking brute.

"Sam," says he, "what's two hundred and fifty dollars, after all? We've got the money. One more night of this kid will send

我等了一个小时，确定这事儿没有任何猫腻，才从树上下来，取了回信，沿着篱笆飞快地跑进树林，又花了半个小时才回到山洞。我打开信，凑到灯前念给比尔听。信是钢笔写的，字迹潦草。大致内容如下：

致两位亡命徒

阁下：

二位索赎来函今已收讫。鄙人自忖阁下要求略高，特提议一二，虽与二位意见相左，但鄙人相信阁下定会接受。二位将犬子送还并付给鄙人二百五十元，我即同意接手小犬。阁下应于子夜前来为宜，因邻里皆知犬子为自行走失，若知悉实为尔等送还而攻击二位，鄙人概不负责。

埃比尼泽·多尔斯特呈上

“简直就是彭赞斯的海盗[①]！”我说，“蛮不讲理——”

我看了一眼比尔，犹豫了一下，又把话咽了回去。他的眼里满是哀求，无论是在不能说话的人脸上还是在会说话的动物脸上，我从未见过这样的神情。

“山姆，”他说，“不就二百五十块钱吗？我们有这个钱。再和那

① 《彭赞斯的海盗》，*The Pirates of Penzance*，美国音乐剧。该剧于1879年12月31日在纽约第五大道剧院首演，受到外界广泛好评。

me to a bed in Bedlam. Besides being a thorough gentleman, I think Mr. Dorset is a spendthrift for making us such a liberal offer. You ain't going to let the chance go, are you?"

"Tell you the truth, Bill," says I, "this little he ewe lamb has somewhat got on my nerves too. We'll take him home, pay the ransom and make our get-away."

We took him home that night. We got him to go by telling him that his father had bought a silver-mounted rifle and a pair of moccasins for him, and we were going to hunt bears the next day.

It was just twelve o'clock when we knocked at Ebenezer's front door. Just at the moment when I should have been abstracting the fifteen hundred dollars from the box under the tree, according to the original proposition, Bill was counting out two hundred and fifty dollars into Dorset's hand.

When the kid found out we were going to leave him at home he started up a howl like a calliope and fastened himself as tight as a leech to Bill's leg. His father peeled him away gradually, like a porous plaster.

"How long can you hold him?" asks Bill.

"I'm not as strong as I used to be," says old Dorset, "but I think I can promise you ten minutes."

"Enough," says Bill. "In ten minutes I shall cross the Central, Southern and Middle Western States, and be legging it trippingly for the Canadian border."

And, as dark as it was, and as fat as Bill was, and as good a runner as I am, he was a good mile and a half out of Summit before I could catch up with him.

孩子多待一天，我肯定会疯掉。多尔斯特先生只向我们要了这价，我觉得他不但是个十足的绅士，还是个慷慨大度之人。你不会放过这个机会的，对吧？”

“说实话，比尔，”我说，“这个小家伙的确让人心烦。那我们就把他送回去，赔点钱好脱身。”

我们当晚便送他回家。我们骗他说，他父亲给他买了支银制步枪和一双鹿皮鞋，又说我们第二天要去猎熊，才终于把他哄上了路。

当我们敲开埃比尼泽家的大门时，正好是午夜十二点。若按最初的计划，此时此刻，本应是我们从树下的纸盒子里取出一千五百块赎金，而现在却成了让比尔数二百五十块交到了多尔斯特的手里。

那孩子发现我们要把他丢在家里，开始号啕大哭，哭声犹如汽笛风琴[①]在演奏，然后像蚂蟥一样抱住比尔的腿不撒手。他父亲如同撕膏药一样一点一点把他拽了下来。

“你能拖住他多久？”比尔问。

“我身体已经大不如前，”老多尔斯特说，“但我还是可以困住他十来分钟。”

“足够了，”比尔说，“十分钟够我穿过中部、南部和西部各州，奔向加拿大边境的了。”

虽然天很黑，比尔很胖，我跑得也很快，但等我追上比尔时，他已经逃离顶峰镇足足有一英里半了。

① Calliope，汽笛风琴，又名蒸汽风琴、蒸汽琴，是一种用水蒸气驱动发音的气鸣乐器。其名字来源于希腊神话中九个缪斯神的首领卡莉欧碧女神。因其声音可以传几公里远，所以常被马戏团用于招揽顾客。此处形容小孩声音很大。

The Green Door[①]
绿房门

① 小说名“The Green Door”，或译为《绿门》《绿的门》《绿色房门》等。这是欧·亨利短篇小说集《四百万》(*The Four Million*)中的一篇。

傍晚在街头散步时，鲁道夫收到了一位黑人派发的两张广告卡，因而误打误撞地敲开了一扇绿色房门，救助了一位三天没有吃饭，几乎饿晕过去的失业女孩。小说中的卡片有两种：一种是牙医广告，另一种是剧院广告。在他人的眼里，卡片的所指非常明确，但在鲁道夫眼里却产生了强烈的暗示：别人的卡片引导他们去治病、看戏，而鲁道夫的卡片却引导他去救人一命。在作者看来，这种暗示来自主人公内心尚存的冒险精神和神秘莫测的冥冥天意。

正如柏拉图所言，人终其一生都在寻找他的另一半。鲁道夫也是如此。黑人两次从人群中选择了他，鲁道夫也由此选择了自己的命运；他敲开了女孩的门，也敲开了自己的新生活。这个女孩就是他“全部精彩辉煌的冒险经历的最终结果”，就是命运对他冒险行为的“最高奖赏”。

小说家貌似在讲一个冒险故事，其实是在讲普通人的命运。在人员混杂的楼房里，惊险与刺激并存，贫困与挣扎同在。走廊昏暗的灯光在照亮一扇绿房门的同时，也遮暗了更多的绿房门。当鲁道夫发现原来有一大片绿房门还在光明之外时，欧·亨利也向读者展示了他娴熟的小说技巧——在这些绿色房门背后，究竟还有多少灵魂在忍受贫穷煎熬，还在守候救她（他）爱她（他）的另一半呢？

Suppose you should be walking down Broadway after dinner, with ten minutes allotted to the consummation of your cigar while you are choosing between a diverting tragedy and something serious in the way of vaudeville①. Suddenly a hand is laid upon your arm. You turn to look into the thrilling eyes of a beautiful woman, wonderful in diamonds and Russian sables. She thrusts hurriedly into your hand an extremely hot buttered roll, flashes out a tiny pair of scissors, snips off the second button of your overcoat, meaningly ejaculates the one word, "parallelogram!" and swiftly flies down a cross street, looking back fearfully over her shoulder.

That would be pure adventure. Would you accept it? Not you. You would flush with embarrassment; you would sheepishly drop the roll and continue down Broadway, fumbling feebly for the missing button. This you would do unless you are one of the blessed few in whom the pure spirit of adventure is not dead.

True adventurers have never been plentiful. They who are set down in print as such have been mostly business men with newly invented methods. They have been out after the things they wanted–golden fleeces, holy grails, lady loves, treasure, crowns and fame. The true adventurer goes forth aimless and uncalculating to meet and greet unknown fate. A fine example was Prodigal Son–when he started back home.

Half-adventurers–brave and splendid figures–have been

① 作者用 diverting（有趣的）修饰 tragedy（悲剧），用 serious（严肃的）修饰 vaudeville（歌舞、杂耍），以营造反讽和幽默效果，称为矛盾修辞（Oxymoron）。这是欧·亨利小说的重要特征之一，本小说多处使用此手法。

假如晚饭后你正沿百老汇大街散步，边打算十分钟内品完一支雪茄，边犹豫是去看妙趣横生的悲剧还是去欣赏严肃庄重的歌舞杂耍。突然有只手搭在你胳臂上。一转身，一位绝代佳人正与你凝眸对视，眼神勾魂摄魄，她一袭俄式黑貂大氅，浑身珠光宝气。她急忙塞给你一只滚烫的奶油卷，亮出一把小剪刀，剪掉你大衣的第二颗纽扣，饱含深意地迸出这个词——“平行四边形”，然后飞也似的穿过路口，紧张兮兮地回头张望着。

这才是真正的冒险。你会接招吗？绝对不会！你会窘得满脸绯红，羞怯地丢掉奶油卷，继续沿百老汇大街前行，一只手无力地摩挲着缺失纽扣的地方。这才是你会做的，除非你是少数几个真正冒险精神尚未泯灭的幸运儿之一。

真正的冒险家历来寥寥无几。印在书里的冒险家多半是些身怀绝技的事业家。他们背井离乡去追求自己想要的东西——金羊毛、圣杯、情人、金银财宝、王位以及名誉。而真正的冒险家从不精于算计，他们五湖四海地游荡，去迎接和拥抱未知的命运。《路加福音》里讲的回头浪子[1]就是这样的典范。

伪冒险家——那些英武显赫的人物——反倒比比皆是。从十

① Prodigal Son,《圣经·新约》中的人物。他挥霍掉自己分得的家产后回家，重新获得了父亲及家人的接纳，喻为忏悔的人，回头浪子。

numerous. From the Crusades to the Palisades they have enriched the arts of history and fiction and the trade of historical fiction. But each of them had a prize to win, a goal to kick, an axe to grind, a race to run, a new thrust in tierce to deliver, a name to carve, a crow to pick–so they were not followers of true adventure.

In the big city the twin spirits Romance and Adventure are always abroad seeking worthy wooers. As we roam the streets they slyly peep at us and challenge us in twenty different guises. Without knowing why, we look up suddenly to see in a window a face that seems to belong to our gallery of intimate portraits; in a sleeping thoroughfare we hear a cry of agony and fear coming from an empty and shuttered house; instead of at our familiar curb a cab-driver deposits us before a strange door, which one, with a smile, opens for us and bids us enter; a slip of paper written upon, flutters down to our feet from the high lattices of Chance; we exchange glances of instantaneous hate, affection, and fear with hurrying strangers in the passing crowds; a sudden souse of rain–and our umbrella may be sheltering the daughter of the Full Moon and first cousin of the Sidereal System; at every corner handkerchiefs drop, fingers beckon, eyes besiege, and the lost, the lonely, the rapturous, the mysterious, the perilous changing clues of adventure are slipped into our fingers. But few of us are willing to hold and follow them. We are grown stiff with the ramrod of convention down our backs. We pass on; and some day we come, at the end of a very dull life, to reflect that our romance has been a pallid thing of a marriage or two, a satin rosette kept in a safe-deposit drawer, and a lifelong feud with a

字军东征到帕利塞德之战[1]，他们既装点了历史传奇，又丰富了小说文艺，还繁荣了出版生意。但是，他们或为赏金，或为赢球，或为砺兵，或为夺冠，或为封喉一剑，或为名扬千秋，或者只为找茬抬杠、约架斗殴——所以都不是冒险的真正追随者。

在大都市里，浪漫和冒险[2]就像一对孪生精灵，总在异国他乡寻觅货真价实的追随者。他们会在我们漫步街头时向我们窥视，会在二十种不同的伪装下向我们挑衅。不知为何，冷不丁一抬头，我们会瞥见窗边有张面孔，仿佛是我们亲友肖像集中的一幅；游走在沉寂的大街上，我们会听到痛苦、恐惧的号叫从门窗紧闭的空房子里传出；出租车司机不会把我们放在熟悉的路牙旁，而是拉到一个陌生的门口，有人满脸堆笑，开门招呼我们进去；途经高耸的“命运”之楼，一张字条会飘然而下，从高高的栅窗口落在我们脚边；在擦肩而过的人群里，我们与陌生的目光碰撞，交换着倏然而至的仇恨、慈爱或者恐惧；一阵疾风骤雨猝然而降——而我们的雨伞可能恰好为嫦娥阿姨的女儿或者织女姐姐的表妹提供遮挡；每个角落都有丢落的手绢，都有勾引的手指，都有纠缠的目光，而那些迷惘的、孤独的、狂喜的、神秘的、险恶的、千变万化的冒险路数会悄悄滑入我们的手掌。不过，我们中极少有人愿意去抓住他们、追寻他们。传统习俗就像一根笔直的通条插入我们的脊背，让我们只能正襟危坐。我们一路向前，终有一天，在过完一段无聊透顶的生活后，我们开始追忆自己的浪漫往事，发现那不过是一两次平淡无奇的婚姻，一朵锁在

① the Crusades，十字军。the Palisades，帕利塞德，指美国纽约州和新泽西州哈德逊河西岸的悬崖峭壁；美国独立战争早期，华盛顿曾险些被包围于此地附近的李堡，后发觉后突围。另据记载，历史上曾有数起决斗事件在此发生，其中最著名的一起是 1804 年发生在亚历山大 · 汉密尔顿（Alexander Hamilton，曾任美国财政部长）与阿龙 · 伯尔（Aaron Burr，时任美国副总统）之间的决斗，汉密尔顿因此丧命。此处用典故并押尾韵（consonance），小说中多次使用此类艺术手法。

② Romance 和 Adventure 两词的首字母均大写，在小说中用作专有名词，指两个精灵，是拟人化（personification）的修辞手法。另外，小说还多次将这两个词作为普通名词使用，与用作专有名词时的意义多有重叠，故分别译为“浪漫”和“冒险”以保持一致。

steam radiator.

Rudolf Steiner was a true adventurer. Few were the evenings on which he did not go forth from his hall bedchamber in search of the unexpected and the egregious. The most interesting thing in life seemed to him to be what might lie just around the next corner. Sometimes his willingness to tempt fate led him into strange paths. Twice he had spent the night in a station-house; again and again he had found himself the dupe of ingenious and mercenary tricksters; his watch and money had been the price of one flattering allurement. But with undiminished ardor he picked up every glove① cast before him into the merry lists of adventure.

One evening Rudolf was strolling along a cross-town street in the older central part of the city. Two streams of people filled the sidewalks–the home-hurrying, and that restless contingent that abandons home for the specious welcome of the thousand-candle-power *table d'hôte.*

The young adventurer was of pleasing presence, and moved serenely and watchfully. By daylight he was a salesman in a piano store. He wore his tie drawn through a topaz ring instead of fastened with a stick pin; and once he had written to the editor of a magazine that "Junie's Love Test," by Miss Libbey, had been the book that had most influenced his life.

During his walk a violent chattering of teeth in a glass case on the sidewalk seemed at first to draw his attention (with a qualm) to a restaurant before which it was set; but a second

① glove（手套），本词可分为 give love，有示爱、浪漫之意。

保险箱底的绢花和一段与暖气片之间的世仇。

鲁道夫·斯坦纳是位真正的冒险家。他极少有哪天晚上是独自窝在家里而不外出寻觅不期的遭遇和惊奇。对他而言，人生最大的乐趣可能就在下一个街角处。有时，他非常乐于试探一下命运之神，却常常被导向诡异的人生之路。他曾两次在警察局里熬过了整宿；他曾几次三番地发觉自己被狡诈的骗子愚弄；他还曾为一次甜言蜜语的诱惑而付出手表与金钱的代价。但他的冒险热情从未衰减，只要有诱惑，他都会照单全收，体验着快乐的冒险人生。

一天傍晚，鲁道夫正沿老城中心的一条穿城街道闲逛。两股人流挤满了人行道——有些人在匆匆地往家赶，另一些不安分的则弃家而出，奔赴千烛辉映的应酬晚宴。

这位年轻的冒险家装扮得赏心悦目，他安静地游逛着，机警地巡视着。白天他是钢琴销售员。他从不用领带针固定领带，而是用黄水晶的领带环把它圈束起来。他曾给一本杂志的编辑写信说，是丽贝小姐写的《朱妮的爱情考验》[1]极大地影响了他的生活。

他正走着，人行道上的一只玻璃箱里传出一阵剧烈的牙齿打战声，把他的注意力（含有一丝厌恶）首先引向了一家饭馆，玻璃箱就放在饭馆门前。他又瞥了一眼，看见饭馆隔壁门口上方高挂着一块

① *Junie's Love Test*,《朱妮的爱情考验》，是1886年出版的一部通俗小说，作者劳拉·琼·丽贝（Laura Jean Libbey，1862—1964），美国人。

glance revealed the electric letters of a dentist's sign high above the next door. A giant negro, fantastically dressed in a red embroidered coat, yellow trousers and a military cap, discreetly distributed cards to those of the passing crowd who consented to take them.

This mode of dentistic advertising was a common sight to Rudolf. Usually he passed the dispenser of the dentist's cards without reducing his store; but to-night the African slipped one into his hand so deftly that he retained it there smiling a little at the successful feat.

When he had travelled a few yards further he glanced at the card indifferently. Surprised, he turned it over and looked again with interest. One side of the card was blank; on the other was written in ink three words, "The Green Door." And then Rudolf saw, three steps in front of him, a man throw down the card the negro had given him as he passed. Rudolf picked it up. It was printed with the dentist's name and address and the usual schedule of "plate work" and "bridge work" and "crowns," and specious promises of "painless" operation.

The adventurous piano salesman halted at the corner and considered. Then he crossed the street, walked down a block, recrossed and joined the upward current of people again. Without seeming to notice the negro as he passed the second time, he carelessly took the card that was handed him. Ten steps away he inspected it. In the same handwriting that appeared on the first card "The Green Door" was inscribed upon it. Three or four cards were tossed to the pavement by pedestrians both

牙医诊所的电子招牌。一位身材魁梧、衣着奇特的黑人，上身穿红色绣花外套，下身着黄色长裤，头戴一顶军帽，正小心翼翼地向乐意伸手的行人散发广告。

鲁道夫对这种牙医广告早已司空见惯。一般来说，即便他路过发牙医广告的人身边也不会让他们的卡片数量有所减少；但是今晚，这位非洲人竟灵巧地将一张卡片塞到他手里，他只好留下并对这个伟大成就报以微笑。

继续往前走了几步后，他漫不经心地瞄了一眼这张卡片。他很诧异，于是他翻过卡片，又饶有兴趣地看了看。卡片的一面是空白，另一面用墨水写了三个字——“绿房门”。接着鲁道夫看见他前面三步远的地方，有位行人把黑人刚发给他的卡片丢在地上。他上前捡起来。卡片上印着牙医姓名、诊所地址以及“牙床”“牙桥”“牙冠”等项目的价格，还有虚头巴脑的“无痛”手术承诺。

这位极富冒险精神的钢琴销售员停在拐角处琢磨了一会儿。然后他横穿大街，走过一个街区，又穿街折回，混入熙熙攘攘的人流中。再经过黑人身边时，鲁道夫假装没留意他，心不在焉地接过递给他的卡片。又走了十几步，他端详起这张卡片。跟第一张卡片的笔迹一模一样，这张上面也写着三个字——“绿房门”。他前身的人行道上还有三、四张行人丢弃的卡片。这些卡片都是空白面朝上。鲁道夫把它们翻过来。每张上面都印着牙医诊所的那套陈词滥调。

following and leading him. These fell blank side up. Rudolf turned them over. Every one bore the printed legend of the dental "parlors."

Rarely did the arch sprite Adventure need to beckon twice to Rudolf Steiner, his true follower. But twice it had been done, and the quest was on.

Rudolf walked slowly back to where the giant negro stood by the case of rattling teeth. This time as he passed he received no card. In spite of his gaudy and ridiculous garb, the Ethiopian displayed a natural barbaric dignity as he stood, offering the cards suavely to some, allowing others to pass unmolested. Every half minute he chanted a harsh, unintelligible phrase akin to the jabber of car conductors and grand opera. And not only did he withhold a card this time but it seemed to Rudolf that he received from the shining and massive black countenance a look of cold, almost contemptuous disdain.

The look stung the adventurer. He read in it a silent accusation that he had been found wanting. Whatever the mysterious written words on the cards might mean, the black had selected him twice from the throng for their recipient; and now seemed to have condemned him as deficient in the wit and spirit to engage the enigma.

Standing aside from the rush, the young man made a rapid estimate of the building in which he conceived that his adventure must lie. Five stories high it rose. A small restaurant occupied the basement.

The first floor, now closed, seemed to house millinery

作为头号捣蛋鬼，冒险精灵几乎无需向鲁道夫这样纯正的追随者召唤两次。可是两次召唤既已完成，探险马上就要开始。

鲁道夫慢慢回到那位大块头黑人身边，他旁边的牙齿箱仍在“咔嗒”作响。这回鲁道夫没再收到卡片。虽然衣着浮夸可笑，可这位埃塞俄比亚人在那里一站就显示出某种原始的、野性的威严，他彬彬有礼地向一些人发着卡片，也任由另一些人自由自在地走过身边。每过半分钟，他就会吟唱一句刺耳、难懂的话语，既像列车员的叽叽咕咕又像大歌剧的咿咿呀呀。这次他不但没发给鲁道夫卡片，而且在鲁道夫看来，他那张油亮的大黑脸似乎抛给了他一个冰冷的、近乎不屑和蔑视的眼神。

这个眼神刺痛了冒险家。他看得出，这是对他迟钝有余、冒险不足的无声谴责。不管卡片上的神秘字眼意味着什么，这位黑人毕竟两次从人群里挑中了他，而现在好像在指责他少勇无谋，不敢涉身这个诡异的谜团。

闪身站到匆匆的人流旁，年轻人迅速对那栋楼房做了一番打量，他猜想他的冒险肯定藏在楼里面。楼房有五层高。地下室是家小饭馆。

一楼现在关着，大概是卖女式帽子、头花或皮草的小店。二楼

or furs. The second floor, by the winking electric letters, was the dentist's. Above this a polyglot babel of signs struggled to indicate the abodes of palmists, dressmakers, musicians, and doctors. Still higher up draped curtains and milk bottles white on the window sills proclaimed the regions of domesticity.

After concluding his survey Rudolf walked briskly up the high flight of stone steps into the house. Up two flights of the carpeted stairway he continued; and at its top paused. The hallway there was dimly lighted by two pale jets of gas–one far to his right, the other nearer, to his left. He looked toward the nearer light and saw, within its wan halo, a green door. For one moment he hesitated; then he seemed to see the contumelious sneer of the African juggler of cards; and then he walked straight to the green door and knocked against it.

Moments like those that passed before his knock was answered measure the quick breath of true adventure. What might not be behind those green panels! Gamesters at play; cunning rogues baiting their traps with subtle skill; beauty in love with courage, and thus planning to be sought by it; danger, death, love, disappointment, ridicule–any of these might respond to that temerarious rap.

A faint rustle was heard inside, and the door slowly opened. A girl not yet twenty stood there white-faced and tottering. She loosed the knob and swayed weakly, groping with one hand. Rudolf caught her and laid her on a faded couch that stood against the wall. He closed the door and took a swift glance around the room by the light of a flickering gas jet. Neat, but

忽明忽灭的电子招牌表明那里是牙医诊所。招牌上面，有千百种语言七扭八拐地指示着看手相的、缝衣服的、教音乐的、治各种疑难杂症的各色人等的驻所。再高一层，垂下的窗帘和窗棂上的白色牛奶瓶明确宣示这里是住户。

一番审视后，鲁道夫脚步轻盈地走上一段高高的石头台阶，进到楼房里。连续爬上两截铺着地毯的楼梯后，他在楼梯尽头停住了脚步。楼道非常昏暗，两盏煤气灯散发着昏黄的光——右边那盏灯离他较远，左边那盏离他近一些。他向近处那盏灯看去，暗淡的光晕下有一扇绿色的房门。刹那间他有些犹豫；这时，他仿佛又看到了那位玩卡片戏法的非洲人脸上轻蔑的冷笑，于是他径直走向那扇绿房门并叩响了它。

开门前流逝的分分秒秒与真正冒险中的急促呼吸相应和。这绿门背后有什么事不可能发生呢！玩兴正浓的赌徒，哄人入彀的无赖，迷恋并幻想被英雄追求的美女；危险、死亡、爱情、失望、嘲讽——其中任一类人都可能来回应这鲁莽的敲门声。

一阵窸窣声隐隐约约地从里面传出来，门慢慢地打开了。一位年龄不到二十岁的女孩站在那儿，脸色惨白，步履蹒跚。她松开门把手，身体虚弱地晃动，一只手在空中摸索着。鲁道夫赶忙扶住她，让她躺在靠墙的一张褪色的旧沙发上。他关上房门，借着摇曳的煤气灯光，迅速扫视了一下房间。很干净，但极贫穷，这就是他看到的情形。

extreme poverty was the story that he read.

The girl lay still, as if in a faint. Rudolf looked around the room excitedly for a barrel. People must be rolled upon a barrel who–no, no; that was for drowned persons. He began to fan her with his hat. That was successful, for he struck her nose with the brim of his derby and she opened her eyes. And then the young man saw that hers, indeed, was the one missing face from his heart's gallery of intimate portraits. The frank, gray eyes, the little nose, turning pertly outward; the chestnut hair, curling like the tendrils of pea vine, seemed the right end and reward of all his wonderful adventures. But the face was woefully thin and pale.

The girl looked at him calmly, and then smiled.

"Fainted, didn't I?" she asked, weakly. "Well, who wouldn't? You try going without anything to eat for three days and see!"

"Himmel[①]!" exclaimed Rudolf, jumping up. "Wait till I come back."

He dashed out the green door and down the stairs. In twenty minutes he was back again kicking at the door with his toe for her to open it. With both arms he hugged an array of wares from the grocery and the restaurant. On the table he laid them–bread and butter, cold meats, cakes, pies, pickles, oysters, a roasted chicken, a bottle of milk and one of red-hot tea.

"This is ridiculous," said Rudolf, blusteringly, "to go without eating. You must quit making election bets of this kind.

① himmel，德语词，意为天空、天堂等，此处用作感叹词。

女孩一动不动地躺着，就像晕过去了一样。鲁道夫紧张地环视着房间想找只水桶。救人得让他趴在水桶上——哦，不，不！那是救淹死的人。他拿起帽子对她扇了几下。居然奏效，由于圆礼帽边沿碰到了她的鼻子，女孩睁开了双眼。这时，年轻人看清了她的面孔，千真万确，肯定是他内心深处亲友肖像集中遗失的那幅。她那清澈的灰色眼眸，娇小的鼻子，骄傲地朝向外面；栗色的头发犹如豌豆藤上的卷须；这大概就是他全部精彩辉煌的冒险经历的最终结果和最高奖赏了。可是这张脸是如此瘦削、苍白，如此让人可怜！

女孩平静地看着他，微微一笑。

"我晕倒了，是吗？"她有气无力地问道。"唉，谁能不晕倒呢？要是三天没饭吃，你试试就知道了。"

"天哪！"鲁道夫大叫一声，跳了起来。"等我回来！"

他冲出绿门，奔下楼梯。二十分钟后，他赶了回来，踢了踢房门叫她打开。他抱着一大堆从食品店和饭馆里买的东西。他把这些东西放到桌上——有黄油面包、冷餐肉、蛋糕、夹心派、豌豆、泡菜、生蚝、一只烧鸡，一瓶牛奶和一杯热红茶。

"真傻！"鲁道夫气冲冲地嚷起来，"三天不吃饭，就是参加竞选你也不能发这样的赌咒！现在晚饭好了。"他搀着她坐到桌边的

Supper is ready." He helped her to a chair at the table and asked: "Is there a cup for the tea?" "On the shelf by the window," she answered. When he turned again with the cup he saw her, with eyes shining rapturously, beginning upon a huge Dill pickle that she had rooted out from the paper bags with a woman's unerring instinct. He took it from her, laughingly, and poured the cup full of milk. "Drink that first," he ordered, "and then you shall have some tea, and then a chicken wing. If you are very good you shall have a pickle to-morrow. And now, if you'll allow me to be your guest we'll have supper."

He drew up the other chair. The tea brightened the girl's eyes and brought back some of her color. She began to eat with a sort of dainty ferocity like some starved wild animal. She seemed to regard the young man's presence and the aid he had rendered her as a natural thing–not as though she undervalued the conventions; but as one whose great stress gave her the right to put aside the artificial for the human. But gradually, with the return of strength and comfort, came also a sense of the little conventions that belong; and she began to tell him her little story. It was one of a thousand such as the city yawns at every day–the shop girl's story of insufficient wages, further reduced by "fines" that go to swell the store's profits; of time lost through illness; and then of lost positions, lost hope, and–the knock of the adventurer upon the green door.

But to Rudolf the history sounded as big as the Iliad or the crisis in "Junie's Love Test."

"To think of you going through all that," he exclaimed.

椅子上，问道："有喝茶的杯子吗？""在窗边的架子上。"她回答道。当他拿了杯子回来时，发现她正在啃一根硕大的腌黄瓜，眼里闪烁着欣喜若狂的光芒。女人的直觉永远正确，她居然从购物袋的最底层把它扒拉了出来！他大笑着，夺走腌黄瓜，然后倒了满满一杯牛奶。"先喝牛奶，"他命令道，"然后你应该再喝点茶，再吃根鸡翅。如果你的状况很好，明天再吃腌黄瓜。现在，要是你允许我来做客的话，那就共进晚餐吧！"

他拖过另一把椅子坐下。一杯热茶下肚，女孩的眼睛恢复了些光彩，脸色也变得红润起来。她像只饥肠辘辘的野兽般大吃大喝起来，既有一丝优雅还有一点野蛮。她好像把年轻人的出现和他提供的援助都当成自然而然的事儿了——这倒不是说她轻视传统礼仪，而是说生活重压赋予了她将人为的条条框框弃诸脑后的权利。可是，在慢慢恢复了些气力，稍稍觉得舒服点之后，她也恢复了一些应有的礼节。接着，她开始讲述自己那些微不足道的小事。相似的故事每天都发生上千次，这座城市对此已无动于衷，她的故事就是其中的一个——一位女店员，工资不高，还常被"罚款"，"罚款"都肥了店主的腰包；然后是生病误了工时，然后是丢了工作，没了希望，再然后——就是这位冒险家叩击绿房门的事儿。

但对鲁道夫来说，这个故事就像《伊利亚特》史诗一般波澜壮阔，就像《朱妮的爱情考验》中的危机一样意义非凡。

"真难想象你竟然遭受了那么多磨难！"他喊道。

"It was something fierce," said the girl, solemnly.

"And you have no relatives or friends in the city?"

"None whatever."

"I am all alone in the world, too," said Rudolf, after a pause.

"I am glad of that," said the girl, promptly; and somehow it pleased the young man to hear that she approved of his bereft condition.

Very suddenly her eyelids dropped and she sighed deeply.

"I'm awfully sleepy," she said, "and I feel so good."

Rudolf rose and took his hat.

"Then I'll say good-night. A long night's sleep will be fine for you."

He held out his hand, and she took it and said "good-night." But her eyes asked a question so eloquently, so frankly and pathetically that he answered it with words.

"Oh, I'm coming back to-morrow to see how you are getting along. You can't get rid of me so easily."

Then, at the door, as though the way of his coming had been so much less important than the fact that he had come, she asked: "How did you come to knock at my door?"

He looked at her for a moment, remembering the cards, and felt a sudden jealous pain. What if they had fallen into other hands as adventurous as his? Quickly he decided that she must never know the truth. He would never let her know that he was aware of the strange expedient to which she had been driven by her great distress.

“是够苦的。”女孩郑重其事地答道。

“你在这个城市里连个亲戚朋友都没有吗？”

“一个也没有。”

“我在这世上也是孑然一身。”稍稍停顿后，鲁道夫说道。

“我很高兴您也这样。”女孩立刻回应道。听到女孩对他的无亲无故表示赞许，年轻人竟感到有一点点幸福。

猛然间她的眼皮耷拉下来，她深深地叹了口气。

“我困极了，”她说，“不过，感觉好多了。”

鲁道夫站起身，拿起帽子。

“那么我该道声‘晚安’了。睡一大觉对你会有好处。”

他伸出手，她握了一下，说了声“晚安”。然而她眼神里的询问是那么明白，那么坦率，那么楚楚可怜，让他不得不用语言来回答她。

“哦，我明天还会再来，看看你过得怎么样。要甩掉我可没那么容易。”

然后，当他走到门口时，好像他来的方式远不如他已来的事实更重要，她问道：“您怎么会来敲我的门？”

他盯着她看了一会儿，想起了那些卡片，突然觉得又嫉妒又心痛。要是那些卡片落到另一个像他一样乐于冒险的人手里会怎样呢？他当即决定要永远向她隐瞒真相。他永远不会告诉她，对于她因穷苦所迫而要的那个古怪的小伎俩[1]，他一清二楚。

① 此时的鲁道夫以为，他收到的两张卡片是女孩与黑人合伙要的伎俩，故有此说。

"One of our piano tuners lives in this house," he said. "I knock at your door by mistake."

The last thing he saw in the room before the green door closed was her smile.

At the head of the stairway he paused and looked curiously about him. And then he went along the hallway to its other end; and, coming back, ascended to the floor above and continued his puzzled explorations. Every door that he found in the house was painted green.

Wondering, he descended to the sidewalk. The fantastic African was still there. Rudolf confronted him with his two cards in his hand.

"Will you tell me why you gave me these cards and what they mean?" he asked.

In a broad, good-natured grin the negro exhibited a splendid advertisement of his master's profession.

"Dar it is, boss," he said, pointing down the street. "But I 'spect you is a little late for de fust act."

Looking the way he pointed Rudolf saw above the entrance to a theatre the blazing electric sign of its new play, "The Green Door."

"I'm informed dat it's a fust-rate show, sah," said the negro. "De agent what represents it pussented me with a dollar, sah, to distribute a few of his cards along with de doctah's. May I offer you one of de doctah's cards, suh?"①

① 小说中黑人讲的英语有浓重的口音，此处有数个单词发音不准，如 dar，'spect，de，fust，dat，sah，pussented，doctah 等，所说的句子也有语法错误。

"我们有位钢琴调音师也住这栋楼,"他说,"我误敲了你的门。"

在绿房门关闭前,他从房间里看到的最后一样东西是她的笑靥。

走到楼梯口,他停下来,好奇地打量了一下四周。接着,他走到走廊另一端,返回后又上了一层,一脸困惑地查探了一圈。他发现楼里的每扇房门都漆成了绿色。

他满腹疑惑地下了楼来到人行道上。那位衣着奇特的非洲人还在。鲁道夫迎面走过去,手里攥着那两张卡片。

"能不能告诉我,你为什么会给我这些卡片,这是什么意思?"他问道。

黑人咧着大嘴、憨厚地露齿而笑,为其雇主的精湛技艺做着精彩的活广告。

"看那儿,老板。"他顺着大街指了指说。"可是,我估摸您赶第一幕恐怕晚了点。"

鲁道夫顺着他手指的方向望去,看到一家剧院的大门,上方耀眼的电子招牌显示着新上演的剧目——《绿房门》。

"我听说这戏很棒,先生。"那个黑人说。"剧场的伙计,给了我一块钱,先生,让我发这些片子,跟牙医的片子一块。我能再给您一张牙医的片子吗,先生?"

At the corner of the block in which he lived Rudolf stopped for a glass of beer and a cigar. When he had come out with his lighted weed he buttoned his coat, pushed back his hat and said, stoutly, to the lamp post on the corner:

"All the same, I believe it was the hand of Fate that doped out the way for me to find her."

Which conclusion, under the circumstances, certainly admits Rudolf Steiner to the ranks of the true followers of Romance and Adventure.

在他居住街区的拐角处，鲁道夫停下来喝了杯啤酒，抽了根雪茄。点着烟走出来后，他扣上外衣扣子，往后推推帽子，对着街角的路灯杆坚定不移地说：

“不管怎样，我相信是命运之手为我指明了找到她的路。”

根据当时的情况，这一结论肯定足以将鲁道夫·斯坦纳归入到浪漫和冒险的真正追随者的行列。

Two Thanksgiving Day Gentlemen
感恩节的两位先生

饱餐归来的流浪汉斯达菲·皮特在公园又遇见了那位熟悉的老先生。连续九年，每逢感恩节老先生都会请他吃饭，想将此变成传统。不忍让老先生伤心的他只好硬着头皮又吃了一顿，最后两人都进了医院。故事虽然短小但意蕴深厚。在1775年独立战争爆发之前，美国一直处于英国的殖民统治之下，本国的经济和文化发展受到了相当严重的制约。建国以后，年轻的美国总是急于摆脱屈辱的历史，迫切地想要确立属于自己的习俗和传统。在这种心态的驱使下，每逢感恩节，所有人都绞尽脑汁地想有所作为。他们中的很多人对感恩节的历史一无所知，也不明白传统的背后需要文化和历史的积淀，只想通过一些虚伪、僵化的仪式来证明自我的价值。于是慈善家们纷纷在这一天救济穷人，老先生不惜忍饥挨饿延续习俗，就连流浪汉斯达菲也认为这一天的好胃口是为他人服务的。欧·亨利用巧妙的情节和讽刺的笔法揭露了公众的愚昧无知和虚伪的社会现实，抨击了急功近利、急于求成的社会风气，同时他也发出了同情与悲哀的感喟。在拜金主义横行的社会中，唯有在感恩节这一天，人们才能抛下疏离和冷漠拉近彼此的距离，给这个物欲横流的世界带来一星半点的温暖，这不得不叫人扼腕叹息。

There is one day that is ours. There is one day when all we Americans who are not self-made go back to the old home to eat saleratus biscuits and marvel how much nearer to the porch the old pump looks than it used to. Bless the day. President Roosevelt gives it to us. We hear some talk of the Puritans, but don't just remember who they were. Bet we can lick 'em, anyhow, if they try to land again. Plymouth Rocks? Well, that sounds more familiar. Lots of us have had to come down to hens since the Turkey Trust got its work in. But somebody in Washington is leaking out advance information to 'em about these Thanksgiving proclamations.

The big city east of the cranberry bogs has made Thanksgiving Day an institution. The last Thursday in November is the only day in the year on which it recognizes the part of America lying across the ferries. It is the one day that is purely American. Yes, a day of celebration, exclusively American.

And now for the story which is to prove to you that we have traditions on this side of the ocean that are becoming older at a much rapider rate than those of England are—thanks to our git-up and enterprise.

Stuffy Pete took his seat on the third bench to the right as you enter Union Square from the east, at the walk opposite the fountain. Every Thanksgiving Day for nine years he had taken his seat there promptly at 1 o'clock. For every time he had done so things had happened to him—Charles Dickensy things that swelled his waistcoat above his heart, and equally on the

这一天是属于我们的。这一天，所有的美国人都会回归故里，吃几块苏打饼干，感叹几句那旧水泵，说它看起来比过去离门廊近多了。感谢这一天。它是罗斯福总统[1]赠予我们的。我们对清教徒[2]有些印象，但已记不清他们是谁。不过要是他们再想靠岸，无论如何都会挨我们一顿狠揍。普利茅斯岩？噢，这就耳熟多了。自从火鸡市场被人垄断之后，许多人只好改吃母鸡。可是华盛顿的某些人还在向垄断者透露感恩节公告的内容。

越橘沼泽以东的那座大城市已经把庆祝感恩节变成了一个习俗。一年之中，唯有在十一月的最后一个星期四，它才承认渡口以外的那部分美国。这一天是完全属于美国人民的。没错，这是独一无二的举国欢庆的一天。

下面要讲的故事意在证明大洋这一头的我们拥有的传统正变得愈加悠久，其变化的速度远快于英国人的。这多亏了我们美国人充沛的活力和积极的进取心。

斯达菲·皮特坐在联合广场东面入口右手边正对着喷泉的第三张长椅上。连续九年，每年的感恩节他都会在一点钟准时坐到这张椅子上。这一坐每回都能给他带来好运，就像查尔斯·狄更斯[3]笔下

① President Roosevelt，1941年，时任美国总统富兰克林·德拉诺·罗斯福将感恩节的日期提前至十一月的第四个星期四，以促进消费。

② Puritans，1620年，英国清教徒为逃离迫害坐船来到美洲大陆，在马萨诸塞州的普利茅斯登陆上岸。清教徒在次年举行欢庆仪式，感激提供无私帮助的印第安人并庆祝庄稼丰收。

③ Charles Dickens（1812—1870），英国大文豪，著有《双城记》（*A Tale of Two Cities*）、《远大前程》（*Great Expectation*）等。

other side.

But to-day Stuffy Pete's appearance at the annual trysting place seemed to have been rather the result of habit than of the yearly hunger which, as the philanthropists seem to think, afflicts the poor at such extended intervals.

Certainly Pete was not hungry. He had just come from a feast that had left him of his powers barely those of respiration and locomotion. His eyes were like two pale gooseberries firmly imbedded in a swollen and gravy-smeared mask of putty. His breath came in short wheezes; a senatorial roll of adipose tissue denied a fashionable set to his upturned coat collar. Buttons that had been sewed upon his clothes by kind Salvation fingers a week before flew like popcorn, strewing the earth around him. Ragged he was, with a split shirt front open to the wishbone; but the November breeze, carrying fine snowflakes, brought him only a grateful coolness. For Stuffy Pete was overcharged with the caloric produced by a super-bountiful dinner, beginning with oysters and ending with plum pudding, and including (it seemed to him) all the roast turkey and baked potatoes and chicken salad and squash pie and ice cream in the world. Wherefore he sat, gorged, and gazed upon the world with after-dinner contempt.

The meal had been an unexpected one. He was passing a red brick mansion near the beginning of Fifth Avenue, in which lived two old ladies of ancient family and a reverence for traditions. They even denied the existence of New York, and believed that Thanksgiving Day was declared solely for Washington Square. One of their traditional habits was to station

的人物一样幸运，使他不仅心花怒放，而且肚里也满满当当。

不过，今天斯达菲·皮特坐在每年的这个约会地点倒像是一种习惯，而不是由于一年一度、如期而至的饥饿。在慈善家们眼里，穷人每隔一年才会遭受一次饥饿的折磨。

皮特当然不饿。他刚刚饱餐归来，撑得只剩下呼吸和挪动的力气。他的眼睛如同两颗发白的醋栗，牢牢地嵌在油灰面具似的肿胀的脸上。他的呼吸短促，外翻的衣领上堆了一圈类似参议员脖子周围的赘肉，时髦感全无。一星期前救济站的好心人刚缝好的外衣扣子像爆米花一样爆开，在四周落了一地。尽管他衣衫褴褛，胸前破旧的衬衫敞开至锁骨，但十一月的微风，夹带着点点雪花，给他送来的只有怡人的凉爽。那顿无比丰盛的大餐让斯达菲·皮特充满了热量，从第一道牡蛎至最后一道葡萄干布丁，（在他看来）包括了世界上所有的烤火鸡、焗土豆、鸡肉色拉、南瓜派和冰淇淋。因此，他坐在长椅上，肚里塞满东西，带着酒足饭饱后的轻蔑注视着眼前的一切。

那是意料之外的一餐。当时他正途经第五大道起点附近的一座红砖瓦房，房里居住着两位老太太，出生于古老的家族，非常敬畏传统。她们甚至不承认纽约的存在，还深信感恩节仅仅是为了纪念华盛顿广场而设立的。她们的家族传统之一就是派一位仆人站在后门口，等待正午钟声敲响后的第一位饥饿的过路人，盛情地款待他一番。斯达菲·皮特去公园时恰好经过那儿，仆人们就将他请进

a servant at the postern gate with orders to admit the first hungry wayfarer that came along after the hour of noon had struck, and banquet him to a finish. Stuffy Pete happened to pass by on his way to the park, and the seneschals gathered him in and upheld the custom of the castle.

After Stuffy Pete had gazed straight before him for ten minutes he was conscious of a desire for a more varied field of vision. With a tremendous effort he moved his head slowly to the left. And then his eyes bulged out fearfully, and his breath ceased, and the rough-shod ends of his short legs wriggled and rustled on the gravel.

For the Old Gentleman was coming across Fourth Avenue toward his bench.

Every Thanksgiving Day for nine years the Old Gentleman had come there and found Stuffy Pete on his bench. That was a thing that the Old Gentleman was trying to make a tradition of. Every Thanksgiving Day for nine years he had found Stuffy there, and had led him to a restaurant and watched him eat a big dinner. They do those things in England unconsciously. But this is a young country, and nine years is not so bad. The Old Gentleman was a staunch American patriot, and considered himself a pioneer in American tradition. In order to become picturesque we must keep on doing one thing for a long time without ever letting it get away from us. Something like collecting the weekly dimes in industrial insurance. Or cleaning the streets.

The Old Gentleman moved, straight and stately, toward

房里沿袭大宅内的传统。

斯达菲·皮特直愣愣地目视前方，十分钟后，他终于想要换个方向瞧一瞧。费了九牛二虎之力，他总算把头稍稍向左转了一点。突然，他的双眼惊恐地迸了出来，呼吸一下子止住，他那穿着破鞋的短脚扭来扭去，把脚下的石子摩擦得沙沙作响。

那位老先生正穿过第四大道朝他坐着的长椅走来。

连续九年的感恩节老先生都会来与坐在这条长椅上的斯达菲·皮特见面。老先生想把它变成一个传统。一连九年，每年的感恩节他都会在这里找到斯达菲，带他去一家餐馆，看着他大吃一顿。这种事在英国自然而然就发生了。但是美国还是个年轻的国家，九年时间不算短了。老先生拥有坚定的爱国热忱，他觉得在为美国开创传统的道路上自己是一位先驱者。要想别具一格，我们就必须坚持做一件事，永不放弃。例如每周收缴几十美分的工伤保险金，或者清扫街道之类的。

老先生庄严地迈向自己正在努力确立的习俗。确实，每年请

the Institution that he was rearing. Truly, the annual feeding of Stuffy Pete was nothing national in its character, such as the Magna Charta or jam for breakfast was in England. But it was a step. It was almost feudal. It showed, at least, that a Custom was not impossible to New Y—ahem!— America.

The Old Gentleman was thin and tall and sixty. He was dressed all in black, and wore the old-fashioned kind of glasses that won't stay on your nose. His hair was whiter and thinner than it had been last year, and he seemed to make more use of his big, knobby cane with the crooked handle.

As his established benefactor came up Stuffy wheezed and shuddered like some woman's over-fat pug when a street dog bristles up at him. He would have flown, but all the skill of Santos-Dumont could not have separated him from his bench. Well had the myrmidons of the two old ladies done their work.

"Good morning," said the Old Gentleman. "I am glad to perceive that the vicissitudes of another year have spared you to move in health about the beautiful world. For that blessing alone this day of thanksgiving is well proclaimed to each of us. If you will come with me, my man, I will provide you with a dinner that should make your physical being accord with the mental."

That is what the old Gentleman said every time. Every Thanksgiving Day for nine years. The words themselves almost formed an Institution. Nothing could be compared with them except the Declaration of Independence. Always before they had been music in Stuffy's ears. But now he looked up at the Old Gentleman's face with tearful agony in his own. The fine snow

斯达菲·皮特吃顿饭这件事上升不到国家局面，不能同英国的《大宪章》和英国人早餐吃果酱这些事相提并论。但是它毕竟迈出了一步。这多少有点旧习气，至少它能证明在纽——哦不！在美国，确立一个习俗并非不可能。

老先生已到花甲之年，又瘦又高，身着一袭黑衣，鼻上架着一副不太稳当的老式眼镜。他的头发比去年更白、更稀疏，走起路来也更加依赖那根弯手柄的多节大拐杖了。

看着这位每年都会出现的恩人逐渐走近，斯达菲喘着粗气颤抖起来，像是某位女士养的一条过胖的哈巴狗遇到一条流浪狗，吓得直哆嗦。他本想飞奔逃走，但就算桑托斯—杜蒙特[①]使尽浑身解数也没法把他和长椅分开。那两位老太太的家仆实在是太尽责了。

“您好，”老先生说，“看到您挺过了一年的风雨，仍然健康地活在这美丽的世上，这真叫我高兴。仅凭这一点，我们就该在这感恩节好好庆祝一番。如果您愿意随我来，朋友，我将请您吃一顿饭，令您体魄强健、精神愉悦。”

老先生每次都说同样的话，连续九年的感恩节都是如此。这些话本身都快变成习俗了。除了《独立宣言》外，没有什么能与之相比。以往，这些话在斯达菲耳中犹如仙弦轻舞。但是此刻，他抬头望着老先生的脸却感到悲从中来，欲哭无泪。雪花落在他布满汗珠

① Santos-Dumont，桑托斯－杜蒙特（1873—1932），巴西发明家、航空发展的先驱者，制成飞艇，进行首次载人动力飞行，后又制成重于空气的航空器和单翼机。

almost sizzled when it fell upon his perspiring brow. But the Old Gentleman shivered a little and turned his back to the wind.

Stuffy had always wondered why the Old Gentleman spoke his speech rather sadly. He did not know that it was because he was wishing every time that he had a son to succeed him. A son who would come there after he was gone—a son who would stand proud and strong before some subsequent Stuffy, and say: "In memory of my father." Then it would be an Institution.

But the Old Gentleman had no relatives. He lived in rented rooms in one of the decayed old family brownstone mansions in one of the quiet streets east of the park. In the winter he raised fuchsias in a little conservatory the size of a steamer trunk. In the spring he walked in the Easter parade. In the summer he lived at a farmhouse in the New Jersey hills, and sat in a wicker armchair, speaking of a butterfly, the ornithoptera amphrisius, that he hoped to find some day. In the autumn he fed Stuffy a dinner. These were the Old Gentleman's occupations.

Stuffy Pete looked up at him for a half minute, stewing and helpless in his own self-pity. The Old Gentleman's eyes were bright with the giving-pleasure. His face was getting more lined each year, but his little black necktie was in as jaunty a bow as ever, and the linen was beautiful and white, and his gray mustache was curled carefully at the ends. And then Stuffy made a noise that sounded like peas bubbling in a pot. Speech was intended; and as the Old Gentleman had heard the sounds nine times before, he rightly construed them into Stuffy's old formula of acceptance.

的额头上仿佛立马就要发出嘶嘶的融化声。老先生却冻得微微发抖，转过身去背对寒风。

斯达菲一直纳闷为什么老先生的语气总是如此伤感。他不知道，这是因为老先生每次说这话时，总希望有个儿子继承他的事业。等他去世之后，他的儿子能继续来到那个老地方，骄傲而坚定地站在下一个“斯达菲”面前，说：“为了纪念我的父亲。”一个习俗就此形成了。

但是老先生没有子嗣。他租住的房间在几座破旧的褐砂石家族老宅之中，宅子位于公园东面几条冷清的大街之间。冬天，他在皮箱大小的小温室里栽上几株灯笼花。春天，他参加复活节的游行。夏天，他搬往新泽西山间的一所农舍，坐在一张柳条安乐椅上，谈论着一种蝴蝶，他希望有朝一日能找到的一种鸟翼凤蝶。秋天，他请斯达菲吃一顿饭。这些都是老先生要做的事。

斯达菲·皮特抬头望了老先生半分钟，内心满是不安、无助和痛苦。行善的快乐却使老先生的双眼炯炯有神。他脸上的皱纹一年比一年多，但那黑色的蝴蝶小领结依旧打得挺括，白衬衣洁净漂亮，灰色的小胡子经过细心的打理翘得格外神气。这时，斯达菲的嘴里发出了一个声音，听起来像是锅里煮的豆子正“咕噜咕噜”冒着泡。他想开口答话。这个声音老先生已经听过九遍，理所当然地认为他在重复那几句老话。

"Thankee, sir. I'll go with ye, and much obliged. I'm very hungry, sir."

The coma of repletion had not prevented from entering Stuffy's mind the conviction that he was the basis of an Institution. His Thanksgiving appetite was not his own; it belonged by all the sacred rights of established custom, if not by the actual Statute of Limitations, to this kind old gentleman who had pre-empted it. True, America is free; but in order to establish tradition some one must be a repetend—a repeating decimal. The heroes are not all heroes of steel and gold. See one here that wielded only weapons of iron, badly silvered, and tin.

The Old Gentleman led his annual protégé southward to the restaurant, and to the table where the feast had always occurred. They were recognized.

"Here comes de old guy," said a waiter, "dat blows dat same bum to a meal every Thanksgiving."

The Old Gentleman sat across the table glowing like a smoked pearl at his corner-stone of future ancient Tradition. The waiters heaped the table with holiday food—and Stuffy, with a sigh that was mistaken for hunger's expression, raised knife and fork and carved for himself a crown of imperishable bay.

No more valiant hero ever fought his way through the ranks of an enemy. Turkey, chops, soups, vegetables, pies, disappeared before him as fast as they could be served. Gorged nearly to the uttermost when he entered the restaurant, the smell of food had almost caused him to lose his honor as a gentleman,

“谢啦，先生。我跟您去，太感谢啦。我真是饿极了，先生。”

饱腹感让斯达菲头脑昏沉，但他仍然确信自己是确立传统时不可或缺的基石。感恩节这一天的好胃口不仅仅属于他个人，就算是不依照目前的诉讼期限[①]，考虑到既定传统中的种种神圣权利，它也同样属于这位早有预约的善良的老先生。没错，美国是一个自由的国家，但是为了确立传统习俗，必须有人充当循环节的角色，或为那个循环的小数。并非所有的英雄都头戴钢盔身披金甲，也有像他一样的英雄，挥舞一两件铁铸锡造的兵器，上头仅仅镀了一层薄银。

老先生带着他每年的受惠者走向南面的那家餐厅，来到那张熟悉的餐桌旁。他们立刻就被认出来了。

“那老家伙又来了。”一个服务生说。“每年感恩节他都要带这个流浪汉来吃饭。”

老先生坐在桌子对面，想象着他这个古老传统的基石，目光闪烁，像颗灰珍珠。桌上堆满了服务员送来的感恩节美食，斯达菲叹了口气，却被误以为是饥饿的叹息，他举起刀叉，决心为自己雕刻一顶不朽的桂冠。

他杀敌时的神勇无人能比。火鸡、排骨、汤、蔬菜、馅饼，刚一端上桌就被逐一歼灭。走进餐厅时他就已经快饱到了极点，食物的味道险些让他丢掉了绅士的尊严，但他仍然像一名真正的骑士一样

① Statute of Limitations，美国法律规定，违法行为的起诉时效为两年，超过时效后，原告无权提起诉讼。

but he rallied like a true knight. He saw the look of beneficent happiness on the Old Gentleman's face—a happier look than even the fuchsias and the ornithoptera amphrisius had ever brought to it—and he had not the heart to see it wane.

In an hour Stuffy leaned back with a battle won.

"Thankee kindly, sir," he puffed like a leaky steam pipe; "thankee kindly for a hearty meal."

Then he arose heavily with glazed eyes and started toward the kitchen. A waiter turned him about like a top, and pointed him toward the door. The Old Gentleman carefully counted out $1.30 in silver change, leaving three nickels for the waiter.

They parted as they did each year at the door, the Old Gentleman going south, Stuffy north.

Around the first corner Stuffy turned, and stood for one minute. Then he seemed to puff out his rags as an owl puffs out his feathers, and fell to the sidewalk like a sunstricken horse.

When the ambulance came the young surgeon and the driver cursed softly at his weight. There was no smell of whiskey to justify a transfer to the patrol wagon, so Stuffy and his two dinners went to the hospital. There they stretched him on a bed and began to test him for strange diseases, with the hope of getting a chance at some problem with the bare steel.

And lo! An hour later another ambulance brought the Old Gentleman. And they laid him on another bed and spoke of appendicitis, for he looked good for the bill.

战斗。他在老先生的脸上看到了助人为乐的幸福，比栽培灯笼花和捕获鸟翼凤蝶时更幸福，他不忍心让这样的神色消失。

一个小时后，斯达菲靠在椅背上，他终于赢得了胜利。

“太谢谢了，先生，”他一边说一边喘，像一根漏气的蒸汽管道，“谢谢您请我吃了这样丰盛的一餐。”

他睁着呆滞的双眼，费力地站起身，径直往厨房走去。服务员将他像转陀螺似的扭过来，为他指引了出门的路。老先生仔细地点出一美元三十美分的银币，留下十五美分的小费。

同往年一样，他们在门口道别，老先生朝南走，斯达菲往北去。

拐过第一个街角，斯达菲站了一分钟。突然，他的一身破衣服像猫头鹰的羽毛一般鼓了起来，裂得粉碎。紧接着他便如同一匹中暑的马，砰然倒地。

救护车到来的时候，年轻外科医生和司机小声咒骂着斯达菲的体重。他的身上没有酒味，没法移交警局，于是斯达菲和他肚里的两顿大餐被一同送进了医院。在那里，他们使他平躺到病床上，检查他得了什么怪病，希望能弄明白这块赤裸的“钢板”[1]到底怎么了。

瞧！一个小时后，另一辆救护车把老先生也送进了医院。他们将他放到另一张病床上，还提到了阑尾炎，因为他看起来应该挺富裕的。

① the bare steel，此处作者把斯达菲比喻成一块赤裸的钢板，用夸张的手法形象地表现他惊人的体重。

But pretty soon one of the young doctors met one of the young nurses whose eyes he liked, and stopped to chat with her about the cases.

"That nice old gentleman over there, now," he said, "you wouldn't think that was a case of almost starvation. Proud old family, I guess. He told me he hadn't eaten a thing for three days."

不一会儿，一位年轻医生碰到一位眼睛令他着迷的年轻护士，便停下来同她聊了几句病人的情况。

“那位体面的老先生，”他说，“你绝对想不到，他差点饿死。我猜他是出身名门吧。他告诉我他三天没吃过一口东西。”

The Last Leaf
最后一片常春藤叶

瘦小体弱的老画家贝尔曼穷困潦倒但很有爱心，为了激起琼西的求生欲望，他顶风冒雨在深夜里为她画下了一片常春藤叶子，让因为得了肺病而奄奄一息的琼西重获新生，自己却受风寒感染了肺病，离开了人世。小说中埋下的伏笔让“欧·亨利式的结局”既在意料之外，又在情理之中。

小说以轻松幽默的方式反映了沉重的现实，体现了欧·亨利“含泪的微笑”的创作特点。贝尔曼用口音很重的英语，颠三倒四地说着醉话，颇有几分可笑。他一心想要画出一幅杰作，带着两位年轻的女孩离开贫民窟，但房间里的画布等了二十五年都还没等到他落下杰作的第一笔。贝尔曼画在墙上的那片叶子救了琼西一命，成了他的杰作，却让他付出了生命的代价。急转的剧情令人唏嘘。为了说明落魄的画家们居住的地方破旧、混乱，小说形象地描述了一位前来此地要账的债主的故事。他在横七竖八的小巷中兜兜转转，猛然发现自己回到了起点，一分钱的账也没要到，十分滑稽。“不着一字，尽得风流”，画家们的贫困窘迫在寥寥数语中被刻画得淋漓尽致，欧·亨利作为“世界三大短篇小说巨匠”的创作功力由此可见一斑。小说还将击倒琼西，夺走贝尔曼性命的肺炎拟人化。“肺炎先生”仿佛成了一位有些淘气的不速之客。他“摸摸这个、碰碰那个”，似乎很无辜。然而，这些轻松活泼的文字背后却是肺炎的肆虐和画家们的贫病交加。类似的苦涩幽默深化了小说对当时社会现实的批判，增强了作家对底层小人物的同情，为欧·亨利的小说增添了艺术魅力。

In a little district west of Washington Square the streets have run crazy and broken themselves into small strips called "places." These "places" make strange angles and curves. One street crosses itself a time or two. An artist once discovered a valuable possibility in this street. Suppose a collector with a bill for paints, paper and canvas should, in traversing① this route, suddenly meet himself coming back, without a cent having been paid on account!

So, to quaint old Greenwich Village the art people soon came prowling②, hunting for north windows and eighteenth-century gables and Dutch attics and low rents. Then they imported some pewter③ mugs and a chafing dish or two from Sixth Avenue, and became a "colony."

At the top of a squatty, three-story brick house Sue and Johnsy had their studio. "Johnsy" was familiar for Joanna. One was from Maine; the other from California. They had met at the table d'hôte of an Eighth Street "Delmonico's," and found their tastes in art, chicory④ salad and bishop sleeves so congenial that the joint studio resulted.

That was in May. In November a cold, unseen stranger, whom the doctors called Pneumonia⑤, stalked about the colony, touching one here and there with his icy fingers. Over on the east side this ravager strode boldly, smiting his victims by scores, but his feet trod slowly through the maze of the narrow and moss-grown "places."

---

① traverse *v.* 穿过　② prowl *v.* 潜行　③ pewter *adj.* 白镴的
④ chicory *n.* 菊黄　⑤ Pharmacopoeia *n.* 药典

华盛顿广场西面的一个小片区里，街道横七竖八，把这里分割成了一条条"烂胡同"。因为这些"烂胡同"，街道生出了各种奇怪的边边角角。七弯八拐的街道时而还和自己交叉。有一回，一位画家发现住在这样的地方也并非一无是处。要是有位讨债的手持账单到这条街上来催缴颜料、画纸和画布钱，会陡然发现自己兜兜转转又回到了起点，一分钱的账也收不到。

之后不久，画家们纷纷出没在这个稀奇而古老的格林尼治村[①]，寻觅那些朝北的窗户、十八世纪的尖顶山墙、荷兰风格的阁楼，以及低廉的房租。然后，他们又从第六大道搜罗了一些白镴杯子和一两只暖锅，这里于是成了"艺术区"。[②]

苏和琼西的画室设在一幢低矮的三层砖房的顶楼。"琼西"是乔安娜的昵称。她俩一个来自缅因州，另一个来自加利福尼亚州。她们是在第八大道的"德尔蒙尼科之家"吃套餐时认识的，交谈中发现彼此艺术趣味相投，而且都喜欢菊苣沙拉和灯笼袖服装，于是一起租了这间画室。

那还是五月的事情。到了十一月，一位冷酷无情，被医生称为"肺炎"的隐形陌生人鬼鬼祟祟地潜入到了艺术区，用他冰冷的手指摸摸这个，碰碰那个。在整个东部，这个掠夺者昂首阔步地前进，让许多鲜活的生命葬身在了他的魔爪之下。但在这些狭窄逼仄、长满青苔，迷宫式"胡同"里，他的脚步慢了下来。

① 格林尼治村，Greenwich village，位于纽约市曼哈顿南部下西区，也被称为"西村"。在19世纪后期和20世纪上中叶，以波希米亚主义首都和垮掉的一代诞生地著称。很多作家、艺术家都曾在此居住或工作过，如马克·吐温、鲍伯·迪伦。

② 这里英文为colony，意为"殖民地，聚居地，聚居人群"等。如French colonies（法国殖民地），the American colony in Paris（聚居巴黎的美国侨民），an artists' colony（聚居的艺术家）。此处译为"艺术区"，指穷画家们聚居的地方。

Mr. Pneumonia was not what you would call a chivalric old gentleman. A mite of a little woman with blood thinned by California zephyrs was hardly fair game for the red-fisted, short-breathed old duffer. But Johnsy he smote; and she lay, scarcely moving, on her painted iron bedstead, looking through the small Dutch window-panes at the blank side of the next brick house.

One morning the busy doctor invited Sue into the hallway with a shaggy, gray eyebrow.

"She has one chance in — let us say, ten," he said, as he shook down the mercury in his clinical thermometer. "And that chance is for her to want to live. This way people have of lining-u on the side of the undertaker makes the entire pharmacopoeia look silly. Your little lady has made up her mind that she's not going to get well. Has she anything on her mind?"

"She — she wanted to paint the Bay of Naples some day." Said Sue.

"Paint? —bosh! Has she anything on her mind worth thinking twice — a man for instance?"

"A man?" said Sue, with a jew's-harp twang in her voice. "Is a man worth — but, no, doctor; there is nothing of the kind."

"Well, it is the weakness, then," said the doctor. "I will do all that science, so far as it may filter through my efforts, can accomplish. But whenever my patient begins to count the carriages in her funeral procession I subtract 50 per cent from the curative power of medicines. If you will get her to ask one question about the new winter styles in cloak sleeves I will promise you a one-in-five chance for her, instead of one in ten."

"肺炎"先生可不是那种我们认为的侠义老绅士。对于一个被加州海风吹得已没有多少血色的弱小女子，他本该手下留情。可是，心狠手辣、气促喘急的"肺炎"先生是蛮不讲理的。他毒手一出，琼西立马倒下。她躺在油漆过的铁床上，几乎动弹不得，目光穿过那扇小小的荷兰式玻璃窗，盯着对面砖房光秃秃的墙面看得入神。

一天早晨，那位忙碌的医生扬了扬他那灰白浓密的眉毛，示意苏到走廊里。

"她熬过去的概率只有——我直说了吧，一成。"医生一边把体温计里的水银柱甩下去，一边说道。"而且，那一成还得看她求生的欲望。要是病人自己生无可恋，灵丹妙药也救不了她。你这位可怜的朋友铁了心认定自己好不了了。她有什么放不下的吗？"

"她——她梦想有一天能去画那不勒斯海湾。"苏说道。

"画画？这算啥！有什么值得她留恋的吗——比如说男人？"

"男人？"苏的声音像单簧口琴声骤然响起。"男人难道就值得——没有，医生，真的没有这回事。"

"嗯，那就不容乐观了，"医生说道，"我只能尽全力，用目前医学所能提供的最佳方式治疗。但是，一旦病人开始琢磨起自己的葬礼上会有几辆马车送殡，药物的疗效就得减半。如果你能设法让她对今年冬天风衣流行什么袖子之类的问题感兴趣的话，我保证她痊愈的概率可以提高到两成，而不是现在的一成。"

After the doctor had gone Sue went into the workroom and cried a Japanese napkin to a pulp. Then she swaggered into Johnsy's room with her drawing board, whistling ragtime.

Johnsy lay, scarcely making a ripple under the bedclothes, with her face toward the window. Sue stopped whistling, thinking she was asleep.

She arranged her board and began a pen-and-ink drawing to illustrate a magazine story. Young artists must pave their way to Art by drawing pictures for magazine stories that young authors write to pave their way to Literature.

As Sue was sketching a pair of elegant horseshow riding trousers and a monocle of the figure of the hero, an Idaho cowboy, she heard a low sound, several times repeated. She went quickly to the bedside.

Johnsy's eyes were open wide. She was looking out the window and counting — counting backward.

"Twelve," she said, and little later "eleven"; and then "ten," and "nine"; and then "eight" and "seven," almost together.

Sue look solicitously out of the window. What was there to count? There was only a bare, dreary yard to be seen, and the blank side of the brick house twenty feet away. An old, old ivy vine, gnarled and decayed at the roots, climbed half way up the brick wall. The cold breath of autumn had stricken its leaves from the vine until its skeleton branches clung, almost bare, to the crumbling bricks.

"What is it, dear?" asked Sue.

"Six," said Johnsy, in almost a whisper. "They're falling

医生离开后，苏回到画室痛哭了一场，泪水把一张日本品牌的餐巾纸都浸成了纸浆。然后，她拿起画板，吹着爵士调，大步流星地走进琼西的房间。

琼西脸朝窗躺着，瘦弱的身体躺在被窝里一动不动。苏以为她睡着了，口哨声戛然而止。

她架好画板，开始为杂志里的一篇故事配钢笔插图。为杂志故事画插图是年轻的画家通往艺术殿堂的必由之路，那些杂志故事则是青年作家通往文学殿堂的必经之途。

苏正在画故事的主人公，一位爱达荷州的牛仔的打扮——时髦的马术比赛用的马裤和单片眼镜，这时她听见了几声轻微的声响。于是，她连忙来到了床边。

琼西的双眼睁得很大，她正盯着窗外数数——倒着数数。

“十二，”她说道，接着是“十一”，然后是“十”，随后是“九”，紧接着几乎同时说出了“八”和“七”。

苏关切地望着窗外。有什么可数的呢？眼前除了空荡荡的、毫无生气的院子，剩下的就是二十英尺外那座砖房的空墙。一株古老的常春藤爬到了半墙高，藤蔓盘根错节，根部腐朽不堪。瑟瑟的秋风将它的叶子打落在地，只剩下裸露的藤蔓紧紧地趴在光秃破败的墙面上。

“数什么呢，亲爱的？”苏问道。

“六，”琼西悄声说道，“它们现在落得越来越快了。三天前还

faster now. Three days ago there were almost a hundred. It made my head ache to count them. But now it's easy. There goes another one. There are only five left now."

"Five what, dear? Tell your Sudie."

"Leaves. On the ivy vine. When the last one falls I must go, too. I've known that for three days. Didn't the doctor tell you?

"Oh, I never heard of such nonsense," complained Sue, with magnificent scorn. "What have old ivy leaves to do with your getting well? And you used to love that vine so, you naughty girl. Don't be a goosey. Why, the doctor told me this morning that your chances for getting well real soon were — let's see exactly what he said — he said the chances were ten to one! Why, that's almost as good a chance as we have in New York when we ride on the street cars or walk past a new building. Try to take some broth now, and let Sudie go back to her drawing, so she can sell the editor man with it, and buy port wine for her sick child, and pork chops for her greedy self."

"You needn't get any more wine," said Johnsy, keeping her eyes fixed out the window. "There goes another. No, I don't want any broth. That leaves just four. I want to see the last one fall before it gets dark. Then I'll go, too."

"Johnsy, dear," said Sue, bending over her, "will you promise me to keep your eyes closed, and not look out the window until I am done working? I must hand those drawings in by to-morrow. I need the light, or I would draw the shade down."

"Couldn't you draw in the other room?" asked Johnsy, coldly.

有将近一百片呢。数得我头都疼了。现在可容易了。又掉了一片。只剩下五片了。”

“五片什么，亲爱的？告诉苏迪吧。”

“叶子。常春藤上的。最后一片落下时，我也得走了。我三天前就知道会是这样。医生没有告诉你吗？”

“哦，你可别瞎说，”苏不以为然，“那些破藤叶和你的病好不好能扯上什么关系？你这家伙，之前太喜欢那株常春藤了。别傻了。告诉你吧，医生早上和我说你很快就会好起来——他原话是这么说的——他说你十有八九能好起来！这么说吧，这概率大到就像在纽约的街头坐电车或者走路时随时可能路过一座新楼一样。现在该喝点汤了，等你喝好，苏迪得继续画画呢。画好卖给编辑，才能有钱给她生病的孩子买红葡萄酒喝，给自己买些猪排解解馋呢。”

“不用给我买酒。”琼西说道，眼睛依然紧盯着窗外。“又掉了一片。不，我不想喝什么汤。只剩下四片了。我要等到天黑前看着最后那片落下来。然后，我也要走了。”

“琼西，亲爱的，”苏俯下身子靠近她，“你能不能答应我先把眼睛闭上，在我画好之前别再朝窗外看了？明天就是交画稿的最后期限。我画画需要光线，要不我就把窗帘放下了。”

“你就不能换个房间吗？”琼西冷冷地问道。

"I'd rather be here by you," said Sue. "Besides, I don't want you to keep looking at those silly ivy leaves."

"Tell me as soon as you have finished," said Johnsy, closing her eyes, and lying white and still as fallen statue, "because I want to see the last one fall. I'm tired of waiting. I'm tired of thinking. I want to turn loose my hold on everything, and go sailing down, down, just like one of those poor, tired leaves."

"Try to sleep," said Sue. "I must call Behrman up to be my model for the old hermit miner. I'll not be gone a minute. Don't try to move 'til I come back."

Old Behrman was a painter who lived on the ground floor beneath them. He was past sixty and had a Michael Angelo's Moses beard curling down from the head of a satyr along with the body of an imp. Behrman was a failure in art. Forty years he had wielded the brush without getting near enough to touch the hem of his Mistress's robe. He had been always about to paint a masterpiece, but had never yet begun it. For several years he had painted nothing except now and then a daub in the line of commerce or advertising. He earned a little by serving as a model to those young artists in the colony who could not pay the price of a professional. He drank gin to excess, and still talked of his coming masterpiece. For the rest he was a fierce little old man, who scoffed terribly at softness in any one, and who regarded himself as especial mastiff-in-waiting to protect the two young artists in the studio above.

Sue found Behrman smelling strongly of juniper berries in his dimly lighted den below. In one corner was a blank canvas

“我想在这和你待一块呀，”苏说，“再说，我也不想让你总瞧着那些讨厌的藤叶。”

“你画好就叫我。”琼西说着，闭上双眼，脸色苍白，安安静静地躺在床上，像一座倒下的雕塑。“我想看到最后一片叶子落下来。我等烦了，也想腻了。我什么都不想管了，只想往下、一直往下飘，像那些可怜的、疲倦的叶子一样往下飘。”

“你睡一会儿吧，”苏说，“我得去把贝尔曼叫上来，为我做隐居老矿工模特。我马上回来。我回来之前你别动。”

老贝尔曼是一位油画家，就住在他们同一单元的底楼。他已年过六十，长着和米开朗基罗的摩西雕像一样的胡子，那卷曲的胡子顺着一颗萨提尔[1]似的头往下长，随着一副小恶魔般的身体飘拂。贝尔曼是个失败的艺术家。他手中的画笔挥动了四十年，却始终被艺术女神拒于千里之外。他一心想要画的杰作至今还没动笔。这几年，他除了偶尔涂抹几幅商业广告画之外，别的什么也没有画过。他还有一份收入微薄的工作——给附近那些请不起专业模特的年轻艺术家当模特。他过度饮用杜松子酒，还会提起他那即将横空出世的杰作。除此之外，他还是个脾气火爆的小老头，谁要是流露出一点柔情，准会被他狠狠地奚落一番，却自认为是只随时待命的獒犬，守护着楼上画室里的两位年轻画家。

在贝尔曼灯光昏暗的陋室里，苏发现他浑身散发着浓烈的杜松子酒味。在角落里的画架上，那块空白油画布等了二十五年，还没

① 这里的 satyr 指古希腊罗马神话中半人半羊的森林之神，直接音译为“萨提尔”。

on an easel that had been waiting there for twenty-five years to receive the first line of the masterpiece. She told him of Johnsy's fancy, and how she feared she would, indeed, light and fragile as a leaf herself, float away, when her slight hold upon the world grew weaker.

Old Behrman, with his red eyes plainly streaming, shouted his contempt and derision for such idiotic imaginings.

"Vass!" he cried. "Is dere people in de world mit der foolishness to die because leafs dey drop off from a confounded vine? I haf not heard of such a thing. No, I will not bose as a model for your fool hermit-dunderhead. Vy do you allow dot silly pusiness to come in der brain of her? Ach, dot poor leetle Miss Yohnsy."①

"She is very ill and weak," said Sue, "and the fever has left her mind morbid and full of strange fancies. Very well, Mr. Behrman, if you do not care to pose for me, you needn't. But I think you are a horrid old — old flibbertigibbet."

"You are just like a woman!" yelled Behrman. "Who said I will not bose? Go on. I come mit you. For half an hour I haf peen trying to say dot I am ready to bose. Gott! dis is not any blace in which one so goot as Miss Yohnsy shall lie sick. Some day I vill baint a masterpiece, and ve shall all go away. Gott! Yes."

Johnsy was sleeping when they went upstairs. Sue pulled the shade down to the window-sill, and motioned Behrman into the other room. In there they peered out the window fearfully

① 本段和紧跟下一段的两段文字都直接引用了贝尔曼的说话内容。贝尔曼举止粗鲁，受教育程度有限，所以他的英语发音很不标准，许多发音都有问题，并且带有浓重的口音。原文较好地体现了这一点。翻译成中文时难以忠实传达原文的会话特点。

有等到贝尔曼的杰作落笔。她把琼西的胡思乱想告诉了他，也说出了她的忧虑，担心她会像叶子一样瘦小和脆弱，如果她的求生欲望越来越弱，真的会像落叶一样飘走。

老贝尔曼红着双眼，老泪纵横地叫嚷着，对琼西的荒诞念头嗤之以鼻。

“啥！”他喊道，“世上还有这样的傻瓜，看到树叶从那该死的藤上掉下来就想死？从来没有听过这样的事。不，我才不要给你做模特，扮那呆头呆脑的傻隐士。你怎么会让她有那么奇怪的想法？唉，可怜的小琼西小姐。”

“她病得很重，很虚弱，”苏说，“高烧烧得她脑子糊涂了，所以全是些乱七八糟的念头。好吧，贝尔曼先生，你不稀罕给我做模特就拉倒。你真是个极其讨厌的老——老啰嗦鬼。”

“你怎么婆婆妈妈的！”贝尔曼大喊道。“谁说不给你做模特了？走吧，我跟你上去。不是说了半天要给你当模特嘛。走！像琼西那样的好姑娘，真不该病倒在这样的地方。总有一天，我会画出一幅杰作，然后我们都离开这破地方。走！说定了。”

他们到楼上时琼西睡着了。苏拉下窗帘，遮住了整个窗台，并示意贝尔曼到隔壁房间去。在那里，他们心惊胆颤地看了一眼窗外的常春藤，然后彼此默默地对望了一眼。冷雨夹杂着雪花下个不停。穿着破旧的蓝色衬衫的贝尔曼装扮成隐居的矿工，坐在了一把翻转过来当石头的烧水壶上。

at the ivy vine. Then they looked at each other for a moment without speaking. A persistent, cold rain was falling, mingled with snow. Behrman, in his old blue shirt, took his seat as the hermit miner on an upturned kettle for a rock.

When Sue awoke from an hour's sleep the next morning she found Johnsy with dull, wide-open eyes staring at the drawn green shade.

"Pull it up; I want to see," she ordered, in a whisper.

Wearily Sue obeyed.

But, lo! After the beating rain and fierce gusts of wind that had endured through the livelong night, there yet stood out against the brick wall one ivy leaf. It was the last one on the vine. Still dark green near its stem, with its serrated edges tinted with the yellow of dissolution and decay, it hung bravely from the branch some twenty feet above the ground.

"It is the last one," said Johnsy. "I thought it would surely fall during the night. I heard the wind. It will fall to-day, and I shall die at the same time."

"Dear, dear!" said Sue, leaning her worn face down to the pillow, "think of me, if you won't think of yourself. What would I do?"

But Johnsy did not answer. The lonesomest thing in all the world is a soul when it is making ready to go on its mysterious, far journey. The fancy seemed to possess her more strongly as one by one the ties that bound her to friendship and to earth were loosed.

The day wore away, and even through the twilight they

第二天一早，只睡了一小时的苏醒过来后发现琼西眼睛睁得很大，目光呆滞地注视着拉下的绿色窗帘。

“把窗帘拉起来，我要看看。”她低声命令道。

心力交瘁的苏照办了。

但是，你瞧！整整一夜的暴风骤雨过后，依然还有一片叶子屹立在砖墙上。这是最后一片藤叶。靠近茎部的地方还是深绿色的，锯齿状的边缘有些枯黄。在离地面二十英尺高的藤蔓上，那片叶子傲然挺立着。

“这是最后一片了，”琼西说，“我原本以为它昨天晚上必定会掉下来。我听到风声了。它今天一定会掉下来，而我也该走了。”

“哎呀，哎呀！”苏把憔悴的脸贴在枕头上说，“就算你不替自己想想，也得替我想想吧。我可怎么办？”

可是琼西没有回答。世界上最孤独的，莫过于一个随时准备开启那神秘而遥远旅途的人。随着联结她和朋友、尘世的纽带逐一松开，那个念头似乎把她控制得越来越牢。

白昼消逝，即使在暮色中她们还能看见那片孤零零的叶子紧贴

could see the lone ivy leaf clinging to its stem against the wall. And then, with the coming of the night the north wind was again loosed, while the rain still beat against the windows and pattered down from the low Dutch eaves.

When it was light enough Johnsy, the merciless, commanded that the shade be raised.

The ivy leaf was still there.

Johnsy lay for a long time looking at it. And then she called to Sue, who was stirring her chicken broth over the gas stove.

"I've been a bad girl, Sudie," said Johnsy. "Something has made that last leaf stay there to show me how wicked I was. It is a sin to want to die. You may bring me a little broth now, and some milk with a little port in it, and — no; bring me a hand-mirror first, and then pack some pillows about me, and I will sit up and watch you cook."

An hour later she said:

"Sudie, some day I hope to paint the Bay of Naples."

The doctor came in the afternoon, and Sue had an excuse to go into the hallway as he left.

"Even chances①," said the doctor, taking Sue's thin, shaking hand in his. "With good nursing you'll win. And now I must see another case I have downstairs. Behrman, his name is — some kind of an artist, I believe. Pneumonia, too. He is an old, weak man, and the attack is acute. There is no hope for him; but he goes to the hospital to-day to be made more comfortable."

The next day the doctor said to Sue: "She's out of danger.

① even chances 指"机会均等","胜负各半"。

在靠墙的藤蔓上。紧接着夜幕降临，北风又肆虐了起来，雨水依然敲打着窗户，顺着低矮的荷式屋檐哗哗往下流。

天刚破晓，冷漠无情的琼西便下令把窗帘拉起来。

那片藤叶依旧在。

琼西躺着盯着它看了很久。然后她叫了一声苏，苏正在煤气炉子上煮鸡汤。

“苏迪，我真是坏透了，”琼西说，“天意留住了最后那片叶子，是想让我明白我有多坏。寻死可是一种罪过。我现在想要喝点鸡汤了，再来点牛奶吧，加点葡萄酒，再——不；还是先给我一面小镜子，再塞几个枕头在我旁边，我要坐起来看你煮吃的。”

过了一小时，她说道：

“苏迪，我真想有一天能去画那不勒斯海湾。”

医生是下午来的。当他离开时，苏找了个借口来到了走廊上。

“有五成希望了，”医生说这话时握住了苏那瘦削、发抖的双手，“只要精心照料，你会赢的。现在我要到楼下去看另一位病人了。贝尔曼，他的名字听着就像个画家。也是肺炎。他年纪大了，身体又虚弱，病得很厉害。他可是好不了了。不过他今天去住院，可以让他少遭点罪。”

第二天，医生对苏说：“她已经脱离危险了。你赢了。现在只要保证营养，悉心看护就好。”

You won. Nutrition and care now — that's all."

And that afternoon Sue came to the bed where Johnsy lay, contentedly knitting a very blue and very useless woollen shoulder scarf, and put one arm around her, pillows and all.

"I have something to tell you, white mouse," she said. "Mr. Behrman died of pneumonia to-day in the hospital. He was ill only two days. The janitor found him the morning of the first day in his room downstairs helpless with pain. His shoes and clothing were wet through and icy cold. They couldn't imagine where he had been on such a dreadful night. And then they found a lantern, still lighted, and a ladder that had been dragged from its place, and some scattered brushes, and a palette with green and yellow colors mixed on it, and — look out the window, dear, at the last ivy leaf on the wall. Didn't you wonder why it never fluttered or moved when the wind blew? Ah, darling, it's Behrman's masterpiece — he painted it there the night that the last leaf fell."

当天下午，苏来到琼西床前，琼西半躺着，安闲地织着一条毫无用处的亮蓝色羊毛披肩。苏伸出一只胳膊连枕头带人一把将她抱住。

“和你说件事，小东西，”她说道，“贝尔曼先生因为肺炎今天在医院过世了。他生病才两天。头一天一早，门卫发现他在楼下那间屋子里疼得没法动弹。他的鞋子和衣服都湿透了，冰凉冰凉的。大家都不知道他在如此恶劣天气的晚上去了哪里。后来，他们发现了一只还亮着的灯笼，一把挪动过的梯子，几只散落在地上的画笔，还有一块调色板，里面调了绿色和黄色的颜料，还有——瞧瞧窗外吧，亲爱的，你看看墙上最后那片常春藤叶。即使刮风它也纹丝不动，你不觉得奇怪吗？唉，亲爱的，这就是贝尔曼的杰作——最后一片藤叶掉落的夜里，他把那片叶子画了上去。”

A Service of Love
爱的奉献

有绘画天赋的乔与颇有钢琴家潜质的迪莉娅一见倾心，很快结为夫妻。婚后两人居住在一间狭小的公寓里，日子清贫但充满快乐。两个人各自追求着自己的艺术之梦，并对未来生活怀有美好的憧憬。但好景不长，由于他们的家庭缺乏经济来源，两个人都无力支付艺术课程的学费。为了成全对方，他们竟不约而同地选择放弃艺术课程的学习，一个去洗衣店熨烫衣服，另一个去机房烧火，打工挣钱想给对方提供学费，并维持生计。与此同时，他们各自编造善意的谎言，让对方相信自己依然追求着艺术之梦。但故事的最后是典型的“欧·亨利式结尾”。迪莉娅意外的烫伤使得真相浮出水面，美丽的谎言不解自破，但由此两个人进一步明白了对方的真心真情。“当一个人热爱艺术时，总会心甘情愿付出一切。”这是故事中的第一句话，也是被反复提及的一句话。对于乔和迪莉娅来说，这里的“艺术”一方面指他们各自挚爱的绘画和音乐艺术，但另一方面，最伟大的“艺术”莫过于他们之间爱的艺术。

在人生的困难时刻，他们义无反顾地选择牺牲自己而去成全对方，让我们看到了他们彼此对爱情的忠贞，以及为爱甘愿牺牲自我的精神。至此，作者原来要颂扬的并非仅仅是男女主人公对艺术的热情，更是他们之间催人泪下的爱情故事。

When one loves one's Art no service seems too hard.

That is our premise. This story shall draw a conclusion from it, and show at the same time that the premise is incorrect. That will be a new thing in logic, and a feat[①] in story-telling somewhat older than the great wall of China.

Joe Larrabee came out of the post-oak flats of the Middle West pulsing with a genius for pictorial art. At six he drew a picture of the town pump with a prominent citizen passing it hastily. This effort was framed and hung in the drug store window by the side of the ear of corn with an uneven number of rows. At twenty he left for New York with a flowing necktie and a capital tied up somewhat closer.

Delia Caruthers did things in six octaves so promisingly in a pine-tree village in the South that her relatives chipped in enough in her chip hat for her to go "North" and "finish." They could not see her f—, but that is our story.

Joe and Delia met in an atelier where a number of art and music students had gathered to discuss chiaroscuro, Wagner, music, Rembrandt's works, pictures, Waldteufel, wall paper, Chopin and Oolong.

Joe and Delia became enamored[②] one of the other, or each of the other, as you please, and in a short time were married—for (see above), when one loves one's Art no service seems too hard.

Mr. and Mrs. Larrabee began housekeeping in a flat. It was a lonesome flat—something like the A sharp way down at the left-

① feat，有"技术、本领、功绩、卓越的手艺"之意，文本中是指"技艺"。
② enamor *v.* 使迷恋

当一个人热爱自己的艺术时，总会心甘情愿付出一切。

那是我们的前提。这个故事将由此得出一个结论，与此同时又证明这个前提是错误的。就逻辑而言，这的确是件新鲜事儿；但就讲故事而言，可能要比中国的万里长城还要古老。

乔·拉腊毕来自盛产星毛栎的美国中西部平原地区，在绘画艺术方面极具天赋。六岁那年，他以镇子上的抽水泵为主题画了一幅图，画中还有镇上的一位名望之士从水泵旁匆匆走过。这幅画被裱好后挂在了药店窗子里，旁边还挂着几束参差不齐排列着的玉米穗。二十岁那年，他只身来到纽约，脖子上系的领带显得飘逸，不过口袋里的钱包却扎得很有点儿紧。

迪莉娅·凯鲁瑟斯从小生活在南方的一个村庄，那儿松林繁茂。她弹钢琴能弹出六个八音阶，表现出很好的潜质。亲戚们纷纷凑钱支持她去"北方"发展，期望她能够"成名"。但他们没有看到她成……而这便是我们所要说的故事。

乔和迪莉娅在一间画室相遇，一群学习艺术和音乐的学生聚集在此，讨论绘画中的明暗对照法、瓦格纳、音乐、伦勃朗的作品、绘画、瓦尔特杜弗、墙纸、肖邦，还有乌龙茶。

乔和迪莉娅相互吸引，或者叫彼此倾心——随你怎么说，很快他们便结婚了——我们将会一起见证（前文中提到的）——当一个人热爱自己的艺术时，总会心甘情愿付出一切。

拉腊毕夫妇在一套公寓里开始了他们的家庭生活。这是套孤零零的公寓——有点儿像钢琴键盘上最左端的A音符。他们生活得很幸福，因为他们不但有自己热爱的艺术，而且还拥有彼此。对于有钱的年轻人，我有个建议——赶紧卖掉你所有的家产，送给贫

hand end of the keyboard. And they were happy; for they had their Art, and they had each other. And my advice to the rich young man would be—sell all thou hast, and give it to the poor—janitor for the privilege of living in a flat with your Art and your Delia.

Flat-dwellers shall indorse my dictum① that theirs is the only true happiness. If a home is happy it cannot fit too close—let the dresser collapse and become a billiard table; let the mantel turn to a rowing machine, the escritoire② to a spare bedchamber, the washstand to an upright piano; let the four walls come together, if they will, so you and your Delia are between. But if home be the other kind, let it be wide and long—enter you at the Golden Gate, hang your hat on Hatteras, your cape on Cape Horn and go out by the Labrador.

Joe was painting in the class of the great Magister—you know his fame. His fees are high; his lessons are light—his high-lights have brought him renown. Delia was studying under Rosenstock—you know his repute as a disturber of the piano keys.

They were mighty happy as long as their money lasted. So is every—but I will not be cynical. Their aims were very clear and defined. Joe was to become capable very soon of turning out pictures that old gentlemen with thin side-whiskers and thick pocketbooks would sandbag one another in his studio for the privilege of buying. Delia was to become familiar and then contemptuous with Music, so that when she saw the orchestra seats and boxes unsold she could have sore throat and lobster in a private dining-room and refuse to go on the stage.

① dictum *n.* 格言，名言 ② escritoire *n.*（法语词）写字台

穷的看门人——这样你就享受这样的特权：与你热爱的艺术以及你的“迪莉娅”[①]居住在公寓里。

住在公寓里的人应该都认同我的格言，他们的幸福是真正的幸福。如果家庭幸福，房子再小也无所谓——大不了将梳妆台翻倒当台球桌用；将壁炉架改造成划船练习架，写字桌用作备用卧室，把脸盆架当作竖式钢琴；如果可能，让房子的四面墙合围在一起，这样你和你的迪莉娅就在中间。但如果家是另外一个样子，那就让它够宽够长——从旧金山的金门大桥进屋，把帽子挂在哈特拉斯岛屿，把披肩挂在合恩角，然后从拉布拉多走出门。

马克斯托是一位声名远扬的画家，乔就在他那儿学画画。他收的学费高，但课程轻松，这两点使得这位老师名声在外。迪莉娅则跟着罗森斯托克学习钢琴——他因弹坏无数琴键而闻名。

只要他们的钱还够用，生活便非常幸福。每个人亦是如此——但我不会愤世嫉俗。小两口的目标非常清晰明确：乔会很快创作出优秀画作，那时在他的画室里，会挤满争相前来购买他作品的老先生们，他们胡须稀薄却腰包鼓鼓。迪莉娅的音乐才艺也会日趋臻熟，足以让她有资本对音乐满不在乎。如果看到管弦乐队和包厢不叫座，她就可以以喉咙痛为由拒绝登台，而去私人餐厅享用龙虾。

① 迪莉娅此处代指“爱人”。

But the best, in my opinion, was the home life in the little flat— the ardent, voluble chats after the day's study; the cozy dinners and fresh, light breakfasts; the interchange of ambitions—ambitions interwoven each with the other's or else inconsiderable—the mutual help and inspiration;and—overlook my artlessness—stuffed olives and cheese sandwiches at 11 p.m.

But after a while Art flagged. It sometimes does, even if some switchman doesn't flag it. Everything going out and nothing coming in, as the vulgarians say. Money was lacking to pay Mr. Magister and Herr Rosen stock their prices. When one loves one's Art no service seems too hard. So, Delia said she must give music lessons to keep the chafing dish bubbling①.

For two or three days she went out canvassing for pupils. One evening she came home elated.

"Joe, dear," she said, gleefully, "I've a pupil. And, oh, the loveliest people! General—General A. B. Pinkney's daughter—on Seventy-First Street. Such a splendid house, Joe—you ought to see the front door! Byzantine② I think you would call it. And inside! Oh, Joe, I never saw anything like it before.

"My pupil is his daughter Clementina. I dearly love her already. She's a delicate thing—dress always in white; and the sweetest, simplest manners! Only eighteen years old. I'm to give three lessons a week; and, just think, Joe! $5 a lesson. I don't mind it a bit; for when I get two or three more pupils I can

① keep the chafing dish bubbling，字面意思是指让火锅保持翻腾、冒泡，此处借指维持生计。

② 拜占庭艺术（Byzantine Art），约5到15世纪中期在东罗马帝国发展起来的艺术风格和技巧。

但在我看来，最幸福的还是在小公寓里的家庭生活——一天学习结束后，两人坐在一块儿聊聊天，享用温馨的晚餐，还有新鲜、清淡的早餐。互相谈论志向——两个人共同的志向，也谈谈其他微不足道的事情——互相帮助和启发，还有——别在意我说句天真的话——晚上十一点钟一起品尝酿水榄和奶酪三明治。

但是没过多久，艺术之路便中止了。很多时候事情的变化是没有任何预兆的。比如平民老百姓常说的入不敷出。现在他们已支付不起马克斯托先生和罗森斯托克的学费了。然而当一个人热爱自己的艺术时，总会心甘情愿付出一切。因此，迪莉娅说她得去教授音乐课来维持生计。

她在外奔波了两三天，四处招揽学生。一天晚上，她兴高采烈地回到家。

"乔，亲爱的，"她激动地说，"我收到了一个学生。还有，哦，那一家子人真好！一位将军——A·B·品克尼将军的女儿——住在第七十一街。多么豪华的房子啊！乔——你应该看看那扇大门！它可能就是你所说的拜占庭风格。哦，还有里面，乔，我真是大开眼界。

我的学生，也就是他的女儿克蕾门蒂娜，我已经真心喜欢她了。这个娇柔的小姑娘——总穿着白色衣服，既甜美又纯朴！她才十八岁。我每周要给她上三节课。你想想，乔，每节课五美元，但是我一点儿不嫌少呢，等我有两到三个学生的时候，我就又可以继续跟着罗森斯托克先生上课了。好了，你别皱眉头啦，亲爱的，我们一起好好享用晚餐吧。"

resume my lessons with Herr Rosenstock. Now, smooth out that wrinkle between your brows, dear, and let's have a nice supper."

"That's all right for you, Dele," said Joe, attacking a can of peas with a carving knife and a hatchet, "but how about me? Do you think I'm going to let you hustle for wages while I philander in the regions of high art? Not by the bones of Benvenuto Cellini! I guess I can sell papers or lay cobblestones, and bring in a dollar or two." Delia came and hung about his neck.

"Joe, dear, you are silly. You must keep on at your studies. It is not as if I had quit my music and gone to work at something else. While I teach I learn. I am always with my music. And we can live as happily as millionaires on $15 a week. You mustn't think of leaving Mr. Magister."

"All right," said Joe, reaching for the blue scalloped vegetable dish. "But I hate for you to be giving lessons. It isn't Art. But you're a trump and a dear to do it."

"When one loves one's Art no service seems too hard," said Delia.

"Magister praised the sky in that sketch I made in the park," said Joe. "And Tinkle gave me permission to hang two of them in his window. I may sell one if the right kind of a moneyed idiot sees them."

"I'm sure you will," said Delia, sweetly. "And now let's be thankful for Gen. Pinkney and this veal roast."

During all of the next week the Larrabees had an early breakfast. Joe was enthusiastic about some morning-effect

“你这样挺好呀，迪莉。”乔说道，用一把切肉刀和一把短柄斧撬开一罐青豆，“但是我呢？你认为我会让你忙于挣钱，自己却自私地继续学习高雅艺术？我在本韦努托·切利尼[①]的尸骨前起誓，绝不会那样做！我想我可以去卖报纸或做铺路工，那样可以挣一两块钱回来。”迪莉娅走上前，搂着他的脖子。

“乔，亲爱的，你别犯傻了。你必须坚持学习。我并没有放弃音乐而去做其他的事情。我边教边学习呢。我一直在与音乐同在。我们每周十五美元的收入，可以活得像百万富翁那样快乐。你千万不要再想着离开马克斯托先生了。”

“好吧，”乔边一边说，一边去拿上面浇有蓝色调味汁的蔬菜，“但我不想要你去教课，这根本不是艺术。不过你干这个，真是让我既钦佩又怜爱！”

迪莉娅说：“当一个人爱着自己的艺术时，总会心甘情愿付出一切。”

“我在公园里画的那张素描，马杰斯托先生称赞我天空画得好，”乔说，“廷克尔允许我把两幅画挂在他的橱窗里。万一哪个有钱的傻瓜刚好想买，我也许能卖掉一幅。”

“我相信你会的。”迪莉娅甜甜地说道。“现在我们一起来感谢品克尼将军和这烤牛肉吧。”

在接下来的一周里，拉腊毕夫妇一大早就吃完早餐。乔在中央

① Benvenuto Cellini，一位意大利文艺复兴时期的金匠、画家、雕塑家、战士和音乐家。

sketches he was doing in Central Park, and Delia packed him off breakfasted, coddled, praised and kissed at 7 o'clock. Art is an engaging mistress. It was most times 7 o'clock when he returned in the evening.

At the end of the week Delia, sweetly proud but languid, triumphantly tossed three five-dollar bills on the 8x10 (inches) centre table of the 8x10 (feet) flat parlor.

"Sometimes," she said, a little wearily, "Clementina tries me. I'm afraid she doesn't practice enough, and I have to tell her the same things so often. And then she always dresses entirely in white, and that does get monotonous. But Gen. Pinkney is the dearest old man! I wish you could know him, Joe. He comes in sometimes when I am with Clementina at the piano—he is a widower, you know—and stands there pulling his white goatee. 'And how are the semiquavers and the demisemiquavers progressing?' he always asks."

"I wish you could see the wainscoting in that drawing-room, Joe! And those Astrakhan rug portieres. And Clementina has such a funny little cough. I hope she is stronger than she looks. Oh, I really am getting attached to her, she is so gentle and high bred. Gen. Pinkney's brother was once Minister to Bolivia.

And then Joe, with the air of a Monte Cristo, drew forth a ten, a five, a two and a one—all legal tender notes—and laid them beside Delia's earnings.

"Sold that watercolor of the obelisk to a man from Peoria," he announced overwhelmingly.

公园作画，积极追求晨间素描的效果。每天早上七点，迪莉娅便会陪他吃完早餐，送上拥抱、赞美和亲吻后送他出门。艺术简直就是个迷人的情妇。他回家时基本上都是晚上七点了。

一周结束了，尽管迪莉娅感到疲倦但也相当自豪，她得意扬扬地把三张五美元的钞票扔在那八英尺宽、十英尺长的客厅里的那张八英寸宽、十英寸长的桌子上。

“有些时候，”她略显疲惫地说，“克蕾门蒂娜挑战我的耐心。我担心她练习不够，同样的事，得反复叮嘱她。而且她总是穿白色衣服，让人觉得不免单调。不过，品克尼将军倒是一个挺可爱的老头！我希望你能认识他，乔。有时，当我在教克蕾门蒂娜练钢琴时，他会前来观看——他是一个鳏夫，你知道吗？——他总站在那儿捋着白色的山羊胡子。‘十六分音符和三十二分音符教得怎么样啦？’他总这样问。”

“我多么希望你能看到他们客厅里的护墙板，乔！还有那些阿斯特拉罕地毯和门帘。克蕾门蒂娜有一点儿小咳嗽，听起来很有点儿怪怪的。我希望她能够比看上去更强健些。哦，我真的很喜欢她，她真的很有教养。品克尼将军的兄弟还当过驻玻利维亚的公使呢。”

随后，乔带着基督山伯爵①的神情——掏出四张钞票，一张十美元、一张五美元、一张两美元、一张一美元——全是合法钞票，他把这些钱和迪莉娅的放到一起。

“方尖石塔那副水彩画卖给了一个皮奥瑞亚人。”乔得意扬扬地宣布。

① 基督山伯爵：大仲马的一部小说名及文中主人公的名字。小说发表于1844年，描写复辟时期遭到陷害而坐了十四年牢的水手寻找宝藏，最后以基督山伯爵身份复仇的故事。

"Don't joke with me," said Delia, "not from Peoria! "

"All the way. I wish you could see him, Dele. Fat man with a woollen muffler and a quill toothpick. He saw the sketch in Tinkle's window and thought it was a windmill at first, he was game, though, and bought it anyhow. He ordered another—an oil sketch of the Lackawanna freight depot—to take back with him. Music lessons! Oh, I guess Art is still in it."

"I'm so glad you've kept on," said Delia, heartily. "You're bound to win, dear. Thirty-three dollars! We never had so much to spend before. We'll have oysters to-night."

"And filet mignon with champignons," said Joe. "Where is the olive fork?"

On the next Saturday evening Joe reached home first. He spread his $18 on the parlour table and washed what seemed to be a great deal of dark paint from his hands.

Half an hour later Delia arrived, her right hand tied up in a shapeless bundle of wraps and bandages.

"How is this?" asked Joe after the usual greetings. Delia laughed, but not very joyously.

"Clementina," she explained, "insisted upon a Welsh rabbit after her lesson. She is such a queer girl. Welsh rabbits[①] at 5 in the afternoon. The General was there. You should have seen him run for the chafing dish, Joe, just as if there wasn't a servant in the house. I know Clementina isn't in good health; she is so nervous. In serving the rabbit she spilled a great lot of it, boiling

① Welsh rabbit :（化开后加入调味品浇在烤面包或脆饼上的）威尔士干酪。这道菜的原名起源于18世纪的大不列颠。

“不要和我开玩笑，”迪莉娅说，“不会是从皮奥瑞亚来的吧！”

“千真万确哦，我希望你能见到他，迪莉。他看起来微胖，围着一条羊毛围巾，嘴里叼着一根羽毛管做成的牙签。他看到廷克尔橱窗里我的那张素描画时，起初还以为是风车，他很果断，不管三七二十一就把它买下来了。他还订购了另一幅——拉克瓦纳货栈的油画——准备带回去。音乐课！哦！我猜想仍有艺术在里面！”

“我很高兴你能这样坚持！”迪莉娅激动地说。“亲爱的，你一定会成功的。三十三美元呢，我们从未有过这么多钱可以支配！今晚我们可以吃牡蛎啦。”

“再来点菲力牛排烧蘑菇。”乔说。“吃橄榄用的叉子放哪儿啦？”

接下来的周六晚上，乔先回到家里。他先把十八美元放在客厅的桌子上，然后洗掉手上大堆黑乎乎的颜料。

半个小时后，迪莉娅也到家了，右手上一堆绷带随意包扎，很不成形。

“你这是怎么了？”乔和往常一样打完招呼后问道。迪莉娅笑了，可不是开心的笑。

“是因为克蕾门蒂娜，”迪莉娅解释说，“上完课后，她执意要吃威尔士奶酪。她也真是古怪，下午五点要吃威尔士奶酪。将军那会儿也在，乔，你是没能看见哦，他连忙跑去拿保温锅，似乎就要亲自动手做的样儿……跟家里没有仆人似的。我知道克蕾门蒂娜的身体不太好；她很容易紧张。她在浇奶酪时弄翻了很多，滚烫滚烫的，溅得我的手及手腕上全是。真是痛得要命，乔。这个可爱的女孩很难过！而且品克尼将军——乔，那个老人几乎吓坏了，他冲到楼下去叫了人——据说是锅炉房或是地下室的什么人——去药店买了

hot, over my hand and wrist. It hurt awfully, Joe. And the dear girl was so sorry! But Gen. Pinkney!—Joe, that old man nearly went distracted. He rushed downstairs and sent somebody—they said the furnace man or somebody in the basement—out to a drug store for some oil and things to bind it up with. It doesn't hurt so much now."

"What's this?" asked Joe, taking the hand tenderly and pulling at some white strands beneath the bandages.

"It's something soft," said Delia, "that had oil on it. Oh, Joe, did you sell another sketch?" She had seen the money on the table.

"Did I?" said Joe, "just ask the man from Peoria. He got his depot to-day, and he isn't sure but he thinks he wants another parkscape and a view on the Hudson. What time this afternoon did you burn your hand, Dele?"

"Five o'clock, I think," said Dele, plaintively. "The iron—I mean the rabbit came off the fire about that time. You ought to have seen Gen. Pinkney, Joe, when—"

"Sit down here a moment, Dele," said Joe. He drew her to the couch, sat beside her and put his arm across her shoulders.

"What have you been doing for the last two weeks, Dele?" he asked.

She braved it for a moment or two with an eye full of love and stubbornness, and murmured a phrase or two vaguely of Gen. Pinkney; but at length down went her head and out came the truth and tears.

"I couldn't get any pupils," she confessed. "And I couldn't

些油膏和其他东西，帮我把手包扎起来，所以现在没那么痛了。”

“那这是什么？”乔继续问道，轻轻地握着她的手，从绷带下抽出了几根白线。

“这是软纱之类的东西，”迪莉娅说，“上面抹了油膏。噢，乔，你又卖掉了一幅素描吗？”她看到了桌子上的钱。

“我吗？”乔说。“你去问问那个皮奥瑞亚人便知道了。他今天取走了那幅画了货栈的画，他有些犹豫，但也许还要买一幅公园风景画或是哈德逊河的风景画。你的手是今天下午什么时候被烫的，迪莉？”

“我想应该是五点钟。”迪莉难过地说。“熨斗——我是说奶酪，大概在那时从炉子上取下来的。你应该看到品克尼将军，乔，当——”

“来这儿坐一会儿，迪莉。”乔说道。他把她拉到沙发上，坐在她的旁边，搂住她的肩膀。

“你在过去的两周里都做了什么，迪莉？”他问道。

她迟疑片刻，眼里充满着爱还有倔强，含糊不清地咕哝了一两个词，是关于品克尼将军的；但最终她还是埋下了头，眼含热泪说出了实情。

“我招不到学生，”她坦白道，“而我也不愿意让你放弃学业，所

bear to have you give up your lessons; and I got a place ironing shirts in that big Twenty-fourth street laundry. And I think I did very well to make up both General Pinkney and Clementina, don't you, Joe? And when a girl in the laundry set down a hot iron on my hand this afternoon I was all the way home making up that story about the Welsh rabbit. You're not angry, are you, Joe? And if I hadn't got the work you mightn't have sold your sketches to that man from Peoria.

"He wasn't from Peoria," said Joe, slowly.

"Well, it doesn't matter where he was from. How clever you are, Joe —and—kiss me, Joe—and what made you ever suspect that I wasn't giving music lessons to Clementina?"

"I didn't," said Joe, "until to-night. And I wouldn't have then, only I sent up this cotton waste and oil from the engine-room this afternoon for a girl upstairs who had her hand burned with a smoothing-iron. I've been firing the engine in that laundry for the last two weeks."

"And then you didn't—"

"My purchaser from Peoria," said Joe, "and Gen. Pinkney are both creations of the same art—but you wouldn't call it either painting or music.

And then they both laughed, and Joe began:

"When one loves one's Art no service seems—"

But Delia stopped him with her hand on his lips. "No," she said— "just 'When one loves.'"

以就在二十四大街的一家洗衣店，找了一份熨衬衫的活儿。关于品克尼将军及克蕾门蒂娜的谎话，我认为自己编造得很好，你认为呢，乔？今天下午，洗衣房的那个女孩不小心把热熨斗放在我手上了，回家的路上我满脑子都在编那个威尔士奶酪的故事。你不会生我的气吧，乔？如果我没有做这份工作，你的素描也不可能卖给那个皮奥瑞亚人。”

“他并不是什么皮奥瑞亚人。”乔吞吞吐吐地说。

“好吧，我不在乎他是哪里人。你太聪明了——乔——快亲亲我，乔——是什么让你怀疑我没有在给克蕾门蒂娜授课？”

“之前我并没有怀疑，”乔说，“一直到今天晚上，因为我今天下午才从机器房里找出棉纱头和油，给了楼上一个被熨斗烫伤的姑娘。这两周我一直在那家洗衣店的锅炉房工作。”

“所以你并没……”

“我的那个皮奥瑞亚买家，”乔说，“和品克尼将军都是同一种艺术的创造物——不过你既不能称其为绘画，也不能称其为音乐。”

他们俩都笑了，乔说：“当一个人热爱着自己的艺术时，总会……”

话还没说完，迪莉娅赶紧用手捂住他的嘴。“不，”她说，“只需说‘当一个人爱的时候。’”

Mammon and the Archer
财神与爱神

理查德深爱着朗崔小姐，却苦于没有机会向她吐露心声。理查德的父亲安东尼家财万贯，认为钱可以买来一切。当他了解到儿子爱而不得的苦恼后，决定施展金钱的魔力，帮助儿子获得向心上人表白的机会。而理查德的姑妈艾伦也给了他一枚古朴别致的戒指，希望能帮助他收获爱情。金钱和戒指？前者代表财神，后者代表爱神，究竟哪个能帮到理查德呢？事实证明，财神竟然更胜一筹。在理查德和朗崔小组坐马车前往剧院的路上，安东尼瞒着儿子和姐姐艾伦，不惜花重金精心打造了一起拥堵事故，让两个年轻人乘坐的马车陷在其中动弹不得，从而帮儿子成功俘获美人芳心。故事的结尾不出意外是典型的“欧·亨利式结尾”，理查德与朗崔小姐来之不易的独处机会，正是他父亲用他最轻蔑的方式——金钱买到的。易得无价宝，难寻有情郎。爱情本应是人类最美好的情感，无关金钱和权力。但是，随着社会不断地发展，缺少了金钱的铺垫，“有情人终成眷属”这样美好的愿景几成奢望。作者将财神与爱神巧妙结合，为读者全面地展现了当时美国人民的爱情观，更是隐晦地表达出对这种现象的无奈，发人深省。

Old Anthony Rockwall, retired manufacturer and proprietor of Rockwall's Eureka Soap, looked out the library window of his Fifth Avenue mansion and grinned. His neighbor to the right—the aristocratic clubman, G. Van Schuylight Suffolk-Jones—came out to his waiting motor-car, wrinkling a contumelious nostril, as usual, at the Italian renaissance sculpture of the soap palace's front elevation.

"Stuck-up old statuette of nothing doing!" commented the ex-Soap King. "The Eden Musee'll get that old frozen Nesselrode yet if he don't watch out. I'll have this house painted red, white, and blue next summer and see if that'll make his Dutch nose turn up any higher."

And then Anthony Rockwall, who never cared for bells, went to the door of his library and shouted "Mike!" in the same voice that had once chipped off pieces of the welkin on the Kansas prairies.

"Tell my son," said Anthony to the answering menial, "to come in here before he leaves the house."

When young Rockwall entered the library the old man laid aside his newspaper, looked at him with a kindly grimness on his big, smooth, ruddy countenance, rumpled his mop of white hair with one hand and rattled the keys in his pocket with the other.

"Richard," said Anthony Rockwail, "what do you pay for the soap that you use?"

Richard, only six months home from college, was startled a little. He had not yet taken the measure of this sire of his, who was as full of unexpectednesses as a girl at her first party.

老安东尼·罗克沃尔，退休前是罗氏尤里卡肥皂公司的制造商兼法人代表。此刻他正在第五大道宅邸的书房，透过窗户往外张望，一幅龇牙咧嘴的样子。他家右邻——贵族俱乐部成员吉·梵·斯凯莱特·萨福克·琼斯——正出了家门，向在外等候的车走去。一如平常，对于耸立在肥皂宫殿正面那座具有意大利文艺复兴时期风格的雕塑，他总是作出嗤之以鼻状。

“真是个狂妄又无用的老东西！”昔日的肥皂大亨说道。“如果他再不加收敛，伊甸蜡像馆早晚会将这个和涅谢尔罗迭一样的外来客收进去！明年夏天我就把这栋房子漆成红、白、蓝[1]三色，到时候再看他的荷兰鼻子还怎样往上翘。”

接着，呼叫仆人时从不按铃的安东尼·罗克沃尔，走出书房，大声叫道：“迈克！”这大嗓门也曾划破堪萨斯大草原的苍穹。

“告诉我儿子，”安东尼吩咐应声而来的仆人，“让他在出门之前到我这儿来一趟。”

小罗克沃尔走进书房，老头将报纸放到一边，抬头看着他，他那光滑而红润的大脸上，神情严肃但也不乏和蔼神情。他一只手揉搓着满头白发，另一只手把口袋里的钥匙弄得叮当作响。

“理查德，”安东尼·罗克沃尔说，“你用的肥皂是什么价？”

理查德从大学毕业才不过六个月，听到父亲的问题感到很惊讶。他至今没摸清父亲的秉性，这老头就像初次参加社交晚会的女孩，总是充满了各种问题。

① 红、白、蓝为荷兰国旗的颜色。

"Six dollars a dozen, I think, dad."

"And your clothes?"

"I suppose about sixty dollars, as a rule."

"You're a gentleman," said Anthony, decidedly. "I've heard of these young bloods spending $24 a dozen for soap, and going over the hundred mark for clothes. You've got as much money to waste as any of 'em, and yet you stick to what's decent and moderate. Now I use the old Eureka—not only for sentiment, but it's the purest soap made.

Whenever you pay more than 10 cents a cake for soap you buy bad perfumes and labels. But 50 cents is doing very well for a young man in your generation, position and condition. As I said, you're a gentleman. They say it takes three generations to make one. They're off. Money will do it as slick as soap grease. It's made you one. By hokey! it's almost made one of me. I'm nearly as impolite and disagreeable and ill-mannered as these two old Knickerbocker gents on each side of me that can't sleep of nights because I bought in between 'em."

"There are some things that money can't accomplish," remarked young Rockwall, rather gloomily.

"Now, don't say that," said old Anthony, shocked. "I bet my money on money every time. I've been through the encyclopaedia down to Y looking for something you can't buy with it; and I expect to have to take up the appendix next week. I'm for money against the field. Tell me something money won't buy."

"For one thing," answered Richard, rankling a little, "it

“爸爸，大概是六美元一打。”

“那你的衣服呢？”

“我想一般是六十美元吧。”

“你是位绅士，”安东尼语气坚定地说，“我也听说过，现在的年轻公子哥们都买二十四美元一打的肥皂，穿的衣服也都在百元以上。你本可以像他们一样花钱如流水，但你始终规规矩矩、节制有度。现在，我用的依然是尤里卡肥皂——不仅仅是因为感情上割舍不下，还因为其品质的纯正。

你若花十多美分买一块肥皂，买到的肯定是劣质的香味和标签。不过，对于你这一代有身份有地位的年轻人来说，用五十美分的肥皂已经够好了。正如我刚所说，你是位绅士。人们说三代才造就一个贵族，他们说的不对，有了钱就有了身份和地位，如同有了油脂肥皂就润滑。钱给了你身份和地位。噢，钱也几乎让我成为上流人物。不过，我简直同住在我们家隔壁的两个荷兰佬一样粗俗、野蛮、不受待见。我把房子买在了他们两个之间，惹得两个老家伙晚上都睡不着觉。”

“有些事有钱也没招，”年轻的罗克沃尔沮丧地说道。

“别这么说，”老安东尼说着，感到震惊，“我坚信我的钱能生钱，我在百科全书中一直搜索到字母 Y 都没找到哪些东西是钱买不到的，下周我再去附录中找找。我相信金钱能搞定一切。告诉我什么东西金钱买不到。”

“比如说，”理查德略带怨气地回答道，“即使有钱也进不了社会

won't buy one into the exclusive circles of society." "Oho! won't it?" thundered the champion of the root of evil. "You tell me where your exclusive circles would be if the first Astor hadn't had the money to pay for his steerage passage over?"

Richard sighed.

"And that's what I was coming to," said the old man, less boisterously. "That's why I asked you to come in. There's something going wrong with you, boy. I've been noticing it for two weeks. Out with it. I guess I could lay my hands on eleven millions within twenty-four hours, besides the real estate. If it's your liver, there's the Rambler down in the bay, coaled, and ready to steam down to the Bahamas in two days."

"Not a bad guess, dad; you haven't missed it far."

"Ah," said Anthony, keenly; "what's her name?"

Richard began to walk up and down the library floor. There was enough comradeship and sympathy in this crude old father of his to draw his confidence.

"Why don't you ask her?" demanded old Anthony. "She'll jump at you. You've got the money and the looks, and you're a decent boy. Your hands are clean. You've got no Eureka soap on 'em. You've been to college, but she'll overlook that."

"I haven't had a chance," said Richard.

"Make one," said Anthony. "Take her for a walk in the park, or a straw ride, or walk home with her from church Chance! Pshaw!"

"You don't know the social mill, dad. She's part of the stream that turns it. Every hour and minute of her time is

名流的圈子。""啊哈！是吗？"这位金钱的拥趸怒气冲冲地吼道。"那你告诉我，如果当初阿斯特的先人们若没有钱买统舱船票来到美国，你所说的社会名流圈又会在哪儿呢？"

理查德叹了叹气。

"这正是我要说的，"老人的语气渐渐平静，"这正是我找你来的原因。孩子，你最近是不是遇到了什么事。两周前我就察觉到了。说给我听听吧，我想，在二十四小时之内，除了房产之外，还可以为你花上一千一百万美元。要是你肝病犯了，咱们的'漫游号'船就停靠在海湾，燃料已备好，两天内便可以送你到巴哈马群岛。"

"你很会猜，父亲大人；您差点就猜对了。"

"啊哈，"安东尼饶有兴趣地问，"她叫什么名字？"

理查德开始在书房里来回踱步。这位老父亲平日里看似大大咧咧，此时却显得极为友好和体贴，儿子忍不住道出实情。

"你怎么不向她表白呢？"老安东尼问道。"她会心甘情愿接受你的。你有钱有相貌，干净体面，从未用过尤尼卡肥皂。你也上过大学，不过她可能不在乎这个。"

"我一直没机会。"理查德说。

"创造个机会，"安东尼说，"约她到公园里散散步，或者驾车去兜兜风，在教堂做完祷告后陪她走回家也可以！哎呀，就这样了啦！"

"您不了解现在的社交界，爸爸。她是能呼风唤雨的人物，她的每时每分都早已提前安排好。我一定要得到这个女孩，爸爸，否则

arranged for days in advance. I must have that girl, dad, or this town is a blackjack swamp forever more. And I can't write it—I can't do that."

"Tut!" said the old man. "Do you mean to tell me that with all the money I've got you can't get an hour or two of a girl's time for yourself?"

"I've put it off too late. She's going to sail for Europe at noon day after to-morrow for a two years' stay. I'm to see her alone to-morrow evening for a few minutes. She's at Larchmont now at her aunt's. I can't go there. But I'm allowed to meet her with a cab at the Grand Central Station to-morrow evening at the 8.30 train. We drive down Broadway to Wallack's at a gallop, where her mother and a box party will be waiting for us in the lobby. Do you think she would listen to a declaration from me during that six or eight minutes under those circumstances? No. And what chance would I have in the theatre or afterward? None. No, dad, this is one tangle that your money can't unravel. We can't buy one minute of time with cash; if we could, rich people would live longer. There's no hope of getting a talk with Miss Lantry before she sails."

"All right, Richard, my boy," said old Anthony, cheerfully. "You may run along down to your club now. I'm glad it ain't your liver. But don't forget to burn a few punk sticks in the joss house to the great god Mazuma from time to time. You say money won't buy time? Well, of course, you can't order eternity wrapped up and delivered at your residence for a price, but I've seen Father Time get pretty bad stone bruises on his heels when

这个城市于我而言永远都只是布满污泥的沼泽地。可是给她写信又不妥，我不能那样做。”

“呸！”老头说，“你的意思是，我用所有的钱都换不来你和这个女孩一两个小时的独处时间？”

“我一拖再拖，来不及了。她后天中午就要出发去欧洲待上两年。明天晚上我过去见上她几分钟。她现在还在拉奇蒙特的姨妈家。我不能去那儿。但是她让我明晚八点半乘车去中央火车站接她。然后我们得迅速赶到百老汇街区的瓦莱克剧院，她妈妈以及一群亲友会在剧院的大厅等着我们。你认为在这种情况下，在六到八分钟里，她会听我表白吗？不会的。在剧院或者是看完演出后我还有什么机会呢？没有。不，爸爸，这是你用钱解决不了的问题。我们不能用金钱买到时间，哪怕只有一分钟；如果可以的话，富人将会活得更长久。看来在朗崔小姐坐船去欧洲之前，我是没希望和她谈一谈了。”

“好吧，理查德，我的孩子，”老安东尼高兴地说，“你现在可以出发去俱乐部了。我很高兴你不是犯了肝病。但是别忘了经常去庙里给财神烧烧高香。你说金钱买不到时间？当然了，永生这个东西你花钱也是买不到的，不可能由人打包好了送上门来。但是我看见时光老人走过金矿时，脚后跟被矿石磨得伤痕累累。”

he walked through the gold diggings."

That night came Aunt Ellen, gentle, sentimental, wrinkled, sighing, oppressed by wealth, in to Brother Anthony at his evening paper, and began discourse on the subject of lovers' woes.

"He told me all about it," said brother Anthony, yawning. "I told him my bank account was at his service. And then he began to knock money. Said money couldn't help. Said the rules of society couldn't be bucked for a yard by a team of ten-millionaires."

"Oh, Anthony," sighed Aunt Ellen, "I wish you would not think so much of money. Wealth is nothing where a true affection is concerned. Love is all-powerful. If he only had spoken earlier! She could not have refused our Richard. But now I fear it is too late. He will have no opportunity to address her. All your gold cannot bring happiness to your son."

At eight o'clock the next evening Aunt Ellen took a quaint old gold ring from a moth-eaten case and gave it to Richard.

"Wear it to-night, nephew," she begged. "Your mother gave it to me. Good luck in love she said it brought. She asked me to give it to you when you had found the one you loved."

Young Rockwall took the ring reverently and tried it on his smallest finger. It slipped as far as the second joint and stopped. He took it off and stuffed it into his vest pocket, after the manner of man. And then he phoned for his cab.

At the station he captured Miss Lantry out of the gadding mob at eight thirty-two.

那天晚上，安东尼正在看晚报，温婉而又多情的艾伦姑妈来了。岁月的洗礼使得她满脸皱纹，而财富的压迫让她唉声叹气。他们开始谈论年轻人的爱情烦恼。

“他把一切都告诉我了，”安东尼说着，打了个哈欠。“我告诉他，我银行账户里所有的钱都可以用来帮他。可他却开始说钱的不是，说有钱也没用。他还说十个百万富翁联合起来也改变不了社会规则。”

“哎，安东尼，”艾伦姑妈叹息道，“我希望你不要把钱想得那么神。真爱是与钱无关的，爱情的力量不可估量。要是他早点说出来就好了！那女孩不可能拒绝我们的理查德。但现在恐怕已经太迟了。他连和她讲话的机会都没有。你所有的财富也不能换来你儿子想要的幸福。”

第二天晚八时，艾伦姑妈从一个封存很久的盒子中取出一枚古朴别致的金戒指，递给了理查德。

“今天晚上戴上它吧，我的侄子，”她央求道，“这是你妈妈给我的。她说这能给爱情带来好运。她托付我说等你有了心上人就交给你。”

小罗克沃尔虔诚地拿着戒指，尝试着戴到小拇指上。这枚戒指滑落到第二个关节处就卡住了。他摘了下来，把它塞进了坎肩兜里，这是男人们的习惯。之后他打电话叫了马车。

八点三十二分时，在火车站熙熙攘攘的人群中，他找到了朗崔小姐。

"We mustn't keep mamma and the others waiting," said she.

"To Wallack's Theatre as fast as you can drive!" said Richard loyally.

They whirled up Forty-second to Broadway, and then down the white-starred lane that leads from the soft meadows of sunset to the rocky hills of morning.

At Thirty-fourth Street young Richard quickly thrust up the trap and ordered the cabman to stop.

"I've dropped a ring," he apologized, as he climbed out. "It was my mother's, and I'd hate to lose it. I won't detain you a minute—I saw where it fell."

In less than a minute he was back in the cab with the ring.

But within that minute a crosstown car had stopped directly in front of the cab. The cabman tried to pass to the left, but a heavy express wagon cut him off. He tried the right, and had to back away from a furniture van that had no business to be there. He tried to back out, but dropped his reins and swore dutifully. He was blockaded in a tangled mess of vehicles and horses.

One of those street blockades had occurred that sometimes tie up commerce and movement quite suddenly in the big city.

"Why don't you drive on?" said Miss Lantry, impatiently. "We'll be late."

Richard stood up in the cab and looked around. He saw a congested flood of wagons, trucks, cabs, vans and street cars filling the vast space where Broadway, Sixth Avenue and Thirty-fourth street cross one another as a twenty-six inch maiden fills

“我们不能让妈妈和其他人等我们。”她说。

“请以最快的速度到达瓦莱克剧院。”理查德按照她的吩咐对车夫说道。

马车从第四十二条街旋风般驶向百老汇，然后穿过一条灯火通明的小巷，就像是从黄昏时分的柔软草地来到了晨光绚丽的山丘。

到了第三十四街，理查德突然猛地用力推开车窗，叫车夫停车。

“我掉了一枚戒指，”他边道歉边下了马车，“那是我母亲的遗物，我不想失去它。我耽误不了多久——我知道它掉在哪儿。”

不到一分钟，他带着戒指回来了。

但就在那一分钟内，一辆跨城小轿车刚好停在了马车前。车夫尝试从左边出去，却被一辆大型邮车给挡住了。车夫又向右拐，可是右边莫名出现了一辆家具搬运车。于是他试着倒车，可是也不行。车夫只好丢掉缰绳，出于职业精神忍不住破口大骂。他的前后左右都被车马堵得严严实实的。

在大城市里，交通堵塞时有发生，让人猝不及防，必然会影响商业或是交通的正常运作。

“为什么不走了？”兰特里小姐焦虑地说道，“我们要迟到了。”

理查德在车厢里站了起来，环顾四周，只见各种货车、卡车、马车、电车都拥堵在百老汇街道、第六大道和第三十四街道交叉处的大片区域，仿佛一个腰围二十六英寸的姑娘强行扎着一根二十二英寸的腰带一样。而且，仍然还有很多车辆从各个交叉路口拼命挤向

her twenty-two inch girdle. And still from all the cross streets they were hurrying and rattling toward the converging point at full speed, and hurling themselves into the struggling mass, locking wheels and adding their drivers' imprecations to the clamor. The entire traffic of Manhattan seemed to have jammed itself around them. The oldest New Yorker among the thousands of spectators that lined the sidewalks had not witnessed a street blockade of the proportions of this one.

"I'm very sorry," said Richard, as he resumed his seat, "but it looks as if we are stuck. They won't get this jumble loosened up[①] in an hour. It was my fault. If I hadn't dropped the ring we—" "Let me see the ring," said Miss Lantry. "Now that it can't be helped, I don't care. I think theatres are stupid, anyway."

At 11 o'clock that night somebody tapped lightly on Anthony Rockwall's door.

"Come in," shouted Anthony, who was in a red dressing-gown, reading a book of piratical adventures.

Somebody was Aunt Ellen, looking like a grey-haired angel that had been left on earth by mistake.

"They're engaged[②], Anthony," she said, softly. "She has promised to marry our Richard. On their way to the theatre there was a street blockade, and it was two hours before their cab could get out of it.

"And oh, brother Anthony, don't ever boast of the power

---

① loosen up, 放松肌肉、松弛、信口开河、慷慨解囊。例："You need to take some exercise to loosen up your muscles." 你需要做些活动以松弛肌肉。

② engaged，使订婚，约定，占用，使卷入，预定，雇佣。通常与介词 in 搭配使用。例："I have never engaged in drug trafficking." 我从来没有从事过贩毒。

这已经是水泄不通的区域，加入这混乱不堪的车阵、马阵中，在原有的喧嚣中，又添进了新的怒吼声。整个曼哈顿的交通仿佛都卡在了这里。成千上万的人站在两边人行道上看热闹，连资历最老的纽约人都不记得何时曾发生过这样的拥堵。

“太抱歉了，”理查德重新坐回到座位上，“我们的马车堵在这里无法动弹了，在一个小时内，这拥挤的交通肯定无法疏通。这都是我的错，要是我没有丢失戒指，我们——”“让我看看戒指吧，”朗崔小姐说道，“现在抱怨也没用，我也不在乎了。本来我也觉得看演出很无聊。”

那天晚上十一点，有人轻敲了安东尼·罗克沃尔的房门。

“进来，”安东尼叫道，他身穿一件红色睡衣，正读着一本海盗历险记。

艾伦姑妈走进来，她的样子仿佛一位滞留人间的白发天使。

“他们订婚了，安东尼，”她柔声说道，“她同意嫁给我们的理查德。他们在去往剧院的路上遇到堵车，过了两个小时才顺利摆脱拥堵。”

“噢，我亲爱的弟弟，不要再鼓吹金钱的力量了。是一个表示

of money again. A little emblem of true love—a little ring that symbolized unending and unmercenary affection—was the cause of our Richard finding his happiness. He dropped it in the street, and got out to recover it. And before they could continue the blockade occurred. He spoke to his love and won her there while the cab was hemmed in. Money is dross compared with true love, Anthony."

"All right," said old Anthony. "I'm glad the boy has got what he wanted. I told him I wouldn't spare any expense in the matter if—"

"But, brother Anthony, what good could your money have done?"

"Sister," said Anthony Rockwall. "I've got my pirate in a devil of a scrape. His ship has just been scuttled, and he's too good a judge of the value of money to let drown. I wish you would let me go on with this chapter."

The story should end here. I wish it would as heartily as you who read it wish it did. But we must go to the bottom of the well for truth.

The next day a person with red hands and a blue polka-dot necktie, who called himself Kelly, called at Anthony Rockwall's house, and was at once received in the library.

"Well," said Anthony, reaching for his chequebook, "it was a good bilin' of soap. Let's see—you had $5,000 in cash."

"I paid out[①] $300 more of my own," said Kelly. "I had to go a little above the estimate. I got the express wagons and cabs

① paid out，付出(钱)，报复，归还。

真爱的信物——一枚象征着天荒地老心永恒的小戒指，帮助理查德找到了他的幸福。他把戒指掉到了街上，便下车去寻找。在他们重新上路前，道路完全被堵住了。于是安东尼向他的心上人表达爱意，俘获了她的一片芳心。和真正的爱情相比，金钱一文不值，安东尼。”

“这很好呀。”老安东尼说道，“我很开心，孩子得到了他喜欢的人。我对他说过，在这件事上，我不会吝啬一分一毫，只要……”

“但是，安东尼弟弟，你的金钱起了什么作用呢？”

“姐姐，”安东尼说道，“海盗现在正处于危险的境地，他的船刚被凿沉，但是他非常清楚金钱的价值，绝不会让自己淹死。我希望你能让我把这章读完。”

故事本该就此结束了。亲爱的读者，我和你们一样，也希望如此。但是，为了一探真相，我们还得继续。

第二天，一个自称凯利的人来找安东尼，他双手通红，系着蓝点领带。安东尼立即在书房接见了他。

“嘿，”安东尼边说着边伸手去拿支票，“这事儿干得真好。让我看看，你已经拿到了五千美元的现金。”

“我自己还垫了三百呢，”凯利说道，“实际支出高出我的估算。快速邮车和单匹马车大多每辆五美元，但是卡车和两匹马拉的车的

mostly for $5; but the trucks and two-horse teams mostly raised me to $10. The motormen wanted $10, and some of the loaded teams $20. The cops struck me hardest—$50 I paid two, and the rest $20 and $25. But didn't it work beautiful, Mr. Rockwall? I'm glad William A. Brady wasn't onto that little outdoor vehicle mob scene. I wouldn't want William to break his heart with jealousy. And never a rehearsal, either! The boys was on time to the fraction of a second. It was two hours before a snake could get below Greeley's statue."

"Thirteen hundred—there you are, Kelly," said Anthony, tearing off a check. "Your thousand, and the $300 you were out. You don't despise money, do you, Kelly?"

"Me?" said Kelly. "I can lick the man that invented poverty."

Anthony called Kelly when he was at the door.

"You didn't notice," said he, "anywhere in the tie-up, a kind of a fat boy[②] without any clothes on shooting arrows around with a bow, did you?"

"Why, no," said Kelly, mystified. "I didn't. If he was like you say, maybe the cops pinched him before I got there."

"I thought the little rascal wouldn't be on hand," chuckled Anthony. "Good-by, Kelly."

② a kind of a fat boy，指罗马神话中的小爱神丘比特，往往被塑造为手拿弓箭、背部长有一对翅膀的调皮胖娃娃。他的金箭射入人心会产生爱情，铅箭射入人心会产生憎恶。

价格提高到了十美元。汽车司机也要十美元，载了人的还要二十。警察要价最高——有两个人我给了五十，其余的给了二十或者二十五美元。场面真够精彩吧，罗克韦尔先生？幸好威廉·阿·布兰迪没有看到马路上车马拥堵成一团的场景。我不想威廉因为嫉妒而伤心。根本没有彩排过。小伙子们都准时到了，分秒不差。整整两个小时堵得连一条蛇都无法钻到格里利的雕像下。”

“这是一千三百美元，拿着吧，凯利。”安东尼说道，撕下了一张支票，“你应得的一千美元，还有你自己垫的三百美元。你不至于鄙视钱吧，凯利？”

“我吗？”凯利说道，“谁发明的贫困，我能揍他。”

安东尼在凯利走出门时叫住了他。

“你注意到了吗？”他说，“在拥堵的时候，一个胖乎乎的光腚男孩正拿着弓箭射向他们。”

“怎么了？没有呀，”凯利说，感到很是莫名其妙，“我没有看见，如果真像你说的那样，可能在我到那之前警察就已经把他给拿下了。”

“我想这个小家伙是不会到场的。”安东尼咯咯地笑出了声，“再见，凯利。”